THEORIZING SOCIAL MOVEMENTS

CRITICAL STUDIES ON LATIN AMERICA
Series Editor: Jenny Pearce
Department of Peace Studies, University of Bradford

Critical Studies on Latin America introduces students
and other readers to the major debates amongst scholars
attempting to theorize political, social and economic
development in Latin America

Surviving in the City:
The Urban Informal Sector in Latin America
Jim Thomas

THEORIZING
SOCIAL MOVEMENTS

Joe Foweraker

Pluto Press
LONDON • BOULDER, COLORADO

First published 1995 by Pluto Press
345 Archway Road, London N6 5AA
and 5500 Central Avenue, Boulder, Colorado 80301, USA

British Library Cataloguing in Publication Data
A catalogue record is available from the British Library

ISBN 0 7453 0713 2 hbk

Library of Congress Cataloging in Publication Data
A catalog record for this book is available from
the Library of Congress

Designed and produced for Pluto Press by
Chase Production Services, Chipping Norton, OX7 5QR
Printed in the EC by WSOY, Finland

Contents

Preface

I wish to thank the friends and colleagues who helped me make this book. Jenny Pearce invited me to write it. Gerry Munck suggested some good theory. Todd Landman encouraged the reading and research. Clare Dekker accompanied and encouraged the writing. Susan Clarke, Todd Landman, Jenny Pearce and Sidney Tarrow commented on the first draft.

I also wish to acknowledge and thank the Economic and Social Research Council for its support of past research in Latin America, and of current research into *Citizenship and Social Movements in Comparative Perspective*. This research, past and present, underpins the argument of the book and informs the analysis throughout.

Friends and colleagues in the Department of Government at the University of Essex have provided constant support and stimulation. All of us who work in the Department benefit from its collegial and creative atmosphere.

Making the book challenged me to combine the in-depth debate of the key analytical issues in the study of social movements with a far-ranging inquiry into social movements in Latin America. It was a challenge I welcomed. I hope you enjoy reading the book as much as I enjoyed making it.

Joe Foweraker
Great Bentley
May 1994

Series Foreword

Theorizing Social Movements is the first of a new series of critical studies on Latin America. The series introduces the reader to the major debates amongst scholars attempting to theorize political, social and economic developments in Latin America as it approaches the millenium.

Economically, the region has been engaged for some years in major structures, changes, opening itself up to highly competitive international markets while tackling the tasks of growth and development in a rapidly changing economic environment. The agency of this development passed in the course of the 1980s from the interventionist state of the postwar decades, to the historically weak private sector, with uneven outcomes in different countries. However, the debate between 'state' and 'market' is by no means over in the region. The urgency of investment in the educational and infrastructural requisites for sustained growth point to a continued role for the state, while a strong state is seen by some as the only means to protect the disadvantaged from the logic of market forces. This logic is transforming labour markets, the relationship between formal and informal economics, the nature of the agrarian sector and the balance between rural and urban development. Persistent tension between growth and equity, wealth creation and poverty alleviation reflect the continued polarization within Latin American societies. Economic transformation and social upheaval reach to the heart of existing class, gender and ethnic relations, creating diverse arenas of challenge and change in these relations. One such arena is politics, where realignments and redefinitions are underway throughout the region. Social movements have challenged the very boundaries of what has hitherto been perceived as 'politics' and the actors associated with it. The role of political parties and political leaders in the relationship between state and society is being reconstructed, albeit in different ways, in many parts of Latin America. Some hail the emergence of a dynamic 'civil society' in the region, while others are more cautious in their analysis of the shifting relationship between the state and its citizens, and between authoritarian and democratic political formations. Latin America, described in the 1960s as a 'living museum' for the way its order has always survived the process of modernization, has entered a new epoch of flux and transition.

This series does not intend to predict outcome nor provide

detailed studies of all aspects of change, but to outline debates and contested approaches in significant areas. The aim is to enrich our understanding of Latin America at one of the region's most dynamic periods of development and to foster discussion on the different ways to conceptualize the processes taking place.

Jenny Pearce, Series Editor
Department of Peace Studies
University of Bradford
January 1995

1 Introduction

The aims of this book are to discover the main debates and issues in contemporary social movement theory, and to discuss their relevance for the study of social movements in Latin America. It does not review the full range of social movement activity in Latin America, but asks how best to approach and understand this activity. Yet the theoretical inquiry does not stand alone; it is illustrated and tested in the present Latin American context. Most empirical reference is to the broad arena of urban social movements, since these are the subject of the largest native literature; and women's mobilization (with or without a feminist content) is treated as thematic, and provides a principle of empirical continuity. But there is no intention of configuring Latin American reality to fit the flickering theoretical images. On the contrary, the theory itself is consistently interrogated to establish its capacity for explaining this reality. Massive social mobilization has occurred across the continent in recent years, but very little social movement theory is made in Latin America.

Social movement theory is necessarily drawn from the experience of particular social movements in particular places, but the present generation has seen an increasing separation of the sites of theoretical production and collective action. Most of the theory has been produced in Western Europe and North America, but, during the past twenty years, this theory has expanded in direct proportion to the decline of their social movements. In the meantime there has been an exponential increase in social movement activity in Eastern Europe, South Africa, China and Latin America. Yet a reading of the theory reveals its universal aspirations. Its broad explanatory claims seek to transcend the geography and history of its own genesis; and there is an attempt to construct a general theory that can travel across the boundaries of time and space. But can this theory truly address the properties of social mobilization in very different political and cultural contexts? In other words, does the theory travel well?

Any response to this question must first recognize that all social movement activity may raise some of the same big questions. Are social movements the same now as in the past? Are they best explained by individual motivation or collective action? What connects the *micro* concerns of social life to the *macro* processes of social change? Above all, should the inquiry begin with *why* or with *how* social actors mobilize? Moreover, can these two questions be treated separately? Since nearly all the theory confronts these questions, and since the questions remain much the same across cultures, it is legitimate to use general social movement theory to explore specific political realities. But the application of the theory must be carefully calibrated. It is doubtful whether Western European or North American theory may be applied directly to the rise of social movements in Latin America, even if many of the same mobilizing issues are seen to recur, albeit in different forms and for different reasons. The task at hand is therefore the graduated one of discovering in what ways and to what degree the theory elucidates Latin American realities.

At the same time it must be recognized that not all the theory is the same. On the one hand, the responses to the big questions combine and intersect differently in different accounts of collective action. On the other, the theory tends to be shaped by its own social and historical context. In Western Europe this included a social democratic consensus, the growth of the welfare state, strong corporatist traditions and a highly institutionalized labour movement. In this context new social movements really did look new, and the theory sought to explain the novelty by major shifts in society and culture. In contrast, the United States had no such social democratic or corporatist traditions, and the labour movement was less important to national politics. There social movements were explained not by big societal changes but by the continuing ability of outsider groups to mobilize resources and gain representation within the system. As a result, the theory contains competing approaches to social mobilization, and the present inquiry must also decide which theory works best for Latin America, or best for different aspects of social movement activity in Latin America.

In Europe the theory has mainly sought to explain why social movements arise in the first place. In doing so it has created a discrete category of new social movements which are understood to express the construction of new social and political identities. Indeed, it is the question of *identity* which has come to define the approach of new social movement theory. In North America, on the other hand, the theory has sought to explain how social actors mobilize, rather than why. Since we are always all more or less equally miserable, why social movements arise seems self-evident. How they do so becomes a double question of how detached individuals make up a social actor, and how some such actors manage to mobilize while others do not; and the theory then develops through an inquiry into resource mobilization, organization, leadership and strategic decision-making. The approach of **resource mobilization theory** is finally defined by its focus on strategy.

This book describes the different variants of these competing approaches in some detail, as well as assessing their strengths and weaknesses; and the argument takes advantage of the tensions between them to reveal key aspects of social movement activity in Latin America. On a priori grounds it appears that the different approaches might best be applied to Latin American movements in a selective and pragmatic fashion. New social movement theory might serve to explain the increasing incidence and broader scope of social mobilization in Latin America, while resource mobilization theory might address the political constraints and opportunities, and explicate the mechanisms of social movement success. Surprisingly, the record shows that it is only new social movement theory which has been applied to Latin America, while resource mobilization theory has been almost entirely ignored. Moreover, the former has often been imported wholesale and applied uncritically, while the latter seems especially appropriate to the analysis of social movements which are a form of mass politics in close and strategic interaction with the state. Hence this book also attempts to redress this imbalance, and achieve a more rounded reading of Latin American social movements.

These comments suggest that social movement theory should be approached with caution, even scepticism. New social movement theory often assumes large processes of historical or societal transformation which remain unproven. Resource mobilization theory makes bold methodological assumptions which offend a sense of cultural context. Both kinds of theory can too easily assume a consensual view of 'normal politics' which provides a benchmark for subsequent definitions; and both kinds of theory are prone to increasing introspection that removes them from the sources and lived experience of social struggle. Where this occurs, the theory is often marred by wishful thinking, and begins to make icons of its object of study. Thus it is remarkable that social movements are nearly always seen as radical and progressive, reflecting an unvoiced assumption that they cannot be anything else. In the Latin American context, by extension, social movements are usually seen as democratic actors, both in practice and in purpose; and if there is scant evidence of democratic activity within the political system, the theory supposes that they are democratizing the society at large. Indeed, what much of the theory lacks is a properly political analysis of the movements, and a realistic assessment of their impact on processes of political change. This requires a more intricate inquiry into their demand-making and into their relationships with other political actors, and especially with the agencies and apparatuses of the state. This is the emphasis pursued in this book.

In this connection, the incursion of new social movement theory into Latin America has discovered a plethora of social movements where none existed before. A wide variety of disparate social phenomena have suddenly been certified by the new social movement label. In some accounts it appears that folk dancers, basket weavers and virtually any form of social or economic life may qualify. But not everything that moves is a social movement; nor can the kind of family, communal or neighbourly activity that has been the stuff of social life for centuries automatically qualify. In fact, in most modern times in most places only a small minority of any population associates civically, and only a handful struggles politically. In contemporary Latin America a large proportion of its populations do not enjoy the minimum material and social conditions for social movement activity, living as they do in physical penury, social deprivation and fear. But even where people have begun to come together in neighbourhood associations or Catholic base communities they are not necessarily engaged in social movement activity, although this kind of associationalism may be considered as *pre-movement*, or as providing the essential social networks and political learning which underpin social mobilization. The social movement itself must then exhibit a sense of collective purpose and the kind of political objectives (construed broadly) which require interaction with other political actors, very often state actors; and, unlike interest groups or NGOs (non-governmental organizations), it must also *mobilize* its supporters in pursuit of its goals. At the other end of the spectrum, social movements stop short of national revolutionary movements, or of armed political movements or insurrections. Nonetheless, social movement activity in Latin America is rarely for the faint-hearted, and often demands a special resilience which can be called heroic.

But it is not simply the theoretical drive to discover social movements in Latin America which makes their definition more difficult today. The first period of mass-based politics in Latin America was that of the populist regimes of the 1930s to the 1960s which sought national industrialization through import-substitution and pursued corporatist policies of labour control. During those years, the range of social movements was relatively limited, and confined to the grand class-based actors like the labour and agrarian movements, with more occasional mobilization by students and teachers. But two major developments, which happened to coincide historically, were to transform this scenario. First, there was the major *lifeworld* shift from rural to urban and industrial society which placed the majority of Latin Americans in a completely different social and political environment. Clearly this shift had been prepared by the industrialization projects, and catalysed by the capitalization of agriculture, but its full demographic and social impact was not felt until the 1970s (when the great majority of Latin Americans were living in cities of more than 100,000 inhabitants). Secondly came the crisis of the populist and developmentalist state (and of the oligarchic state in Central America), and the advent of the repressive military and authoritarian regimes of the 1970s and 1980s. Linking the two developments was the huge growth of the state apparatus, and the massive increase in forms of state intervention in countries like Brazil and Mexico.

These developments had a dramatic impact on social movement activity in Latin America. The previous predominance of class-based movements was complicated by the rise of urban social movements, a catch-all category which includes a wide range of popular political initiatives, usually inspired by demands for public utilities, social services, or access to land and water. At the same time the state became the object of, or was a direct party to, a wide range of social struggles and political demands and, in its military and authoritarian phase, acted to suppress such struggles and demands. In this context, the rise of urban social movements is seen both as a response to the precarious conditions of urban life, and as a response to the repressive policies of the state and the suppression of more traditional forms of political organization, such as political parties and trade unions. None of this is meant to suggest that labour and agrarian movements suddenly disappeared. On the contrary, the labour movement sometimes took on a new salience in opposition to the military regimes (or to the authoritarian regime in Mexico). But the combination of urban expansion and repressive government did prove a fecund context for the emergence of new social actors, especially women; for the discovery of new forms of organization and new strategic initiatives; and for the increasing statement of demands in terms of *rights* that became widespread throughout Latin America from the 1970s onwards.

It was the urban social movements which became the main focus of social movement research and writing in Latin America during the 1970s and early 1980s. In large degree this was because they appeared to represent an authentically popular response to state repression and economic austerity and, consequently, some accounts took on chiliastic overtones. Urban movements were an open-ended category which, depending on time, place and circumstances, could include new forms of the labour movement, women's movements, teachers' movements, student movements and movements on behalf of the 'disappeared' and exiled. But all the movements, as well as agrarian and ethnic movements in the countryside, began to state their demands as rights: land rights, labour rights, educational rights, human rights. The urban context became especially important because of the concentration of movements, and because it seemed to contain the possibility of civil society. Indeed, the spread of more or less autonomous forms of associational activity, linked to a language of rights, could be understood as the (re)creation of that society.

It may be objected that civil society is not simply equivalent to social movement activity, and this is correct. In fact, any complex and 'layered' definition of civil society will include economic (market), legal and political (public sphere), and social (associational) dimensions. At the very least, therefore, an empirical account of civil society will include private sector (business and commercial) interests, a wide range of non-state institutions, and multiform associational activity. But in the Latin America of the 1970s, civil society was seen as a uniquely popular possibility. The state had often crushed trade unions, banned political parties and invaded the universities. There was no freedom of assembly, speech or information, or even habeas corpus. Society had been demobilized. Hence in Mexico the surge of social movement activity was seen as a sign of 'society getting organized', while in Brazil it was said that 'if civil society did not exist it had to be invented'. In short, social movements are not equivalent to civil society, but they were seen as participating in the process of constructing that society, or of recovering it from the state.

For this reason, much of the writing and theorizing of social movements in Latin America was stated in terms of the division between state and civil society. In this regard it must be emphasized that both European and North American theory tend to assume the presence of a dense, articulate and communicative civil society (as well as the dissemination of liberal values within this society), just as they tend to assume liberal democratic regimes. Social movements are then seen as vindicating or protecting particular, delimited and specific sets of rights (since universal rights are guaranteed by the liberal polity). But neither the liberal regime nor the civil society can be taken for granted in the Latin American context, where social movements have had to press for universal rights, and where common civil liberties remain a central concern. There is a radical difference between contexts where citizenship is enshrined and others where its elements are still inchoate.

From this point the debate over civil society in Latin America merges imperceptibly into the debate over democracy and democratization; and social movements themselves become increasingly concerned, both in theory and in practice, with their projection into *political society*, or the arena of political competition for control over public power and the state apparatus. Under authoritarian regimes it is all too evident that this political society must itself be reconstituted by constitutional norms and electoral rules which guarantee freedom of speech and association, and provide for political representation and legislative procedure. There is no doubt that the re-emergence or deepening of political society varies widely between different regimes and within different processes of democratic transition. But there have been few concerted attempts to describe the difficult projection of social movements into political society, or to analyse the contribution of social movements to the many democratic transitions that have taken place in Latin America in recent years. Indeed, there is a sharp divide between the bulk of the social movement literature and the huge new literature on democratic transitions, and this has tended to produce an imbalanced and elite-centred view of the process of democratization. This book attempts to redress this imbalance in some degree, and to restore a sense of the political achievements of social movements.

These themes provide all the elements required for a thumbnail sketch of the contents of this book. Although the following four chapters can stand alone, and can therefore be read in any order without the reader's suffering a complete loss of bearings, they are best read as a developing argument on social movements in Latin America. The argument begins with a careful examination of the theoretical premises, and then moves steadily into contemporary Latin America, and so the Latin American 'content' increases as the argument advances.

Chapter 2, 'Theories of Social Movements', considers both new social movement theory and resource mobilization theory, in that order. Discussion of the first theory includes the debate over the 'newness' of new social movements and the central question of social identities. Resource mobilization theory is described in its different variants, all of which focus on the question of strategy. The argument then recounts the attempts to synthesize the two approaches through the development of the concept of civil society. The theories are examined for their relevance to Latin America, with emphasis on the most salient contextual differences between Europe, North America and Latin America, in regard to forms of state, regime and civil society.

Chapter 3, 'The Sociology of Social Movements', begins with the relationship between class analysis and social movement theory, which prepares the ground for a discussion of definitions of social movements and a return to the debate over 'new' and 'old' movements. The process of construction of identities is analysed in some detail, with illustration from the women's movement in Latin America. The focus throughout is on social movements in civil society.

Chapter 4, 'The Politics of Social Movements', considers the political scope of social movements, and their linkages to the political system, including both the state and political parties. The mutual influence of the state and social movements is debated, with extensive reference to social movements in Latin America in general, and the women's movement in particular. Emphasis is given to the neglected topic of the institutional context of social mobilization, and the focus throughout is on the relationship of social movements to the state.

Chapter 5, 'Social Movements and Democratic Transitions', looks at the political role of social movements in civil society and their projection into political society through the dual process of mobilization and negotiation. This entails a discussion of rights, citizenship and democratic transitions which concludes with some observations on the eventual decline of social movements. A fairly wide range of empirical reference again includes the women's movement. The focus throughout is on the relationship between social movements and citizenship.

2 Theories of Social Movements

This study of social movements in Latin America begins with an account of the two main attempts to construct a general theory of social movements, the European new social movements theory and the North American resource mobilization theory. Both sets of theory emerged in self-conscious reaction to previous models of social scientific analysis: new social movement theory was born of disenchantment with a highly academic and structural version of Marxism; and resource mobilization theory clearly rejected the psychological reductionism of prior theories of collective action in the United States. In addition, both sets of theory emerged in response to the upsurge of social movement activity in the 1960s: the civil rights movement, the women's movement and the anti-war movement in the United States; the student movement, the peace movement, the anti-nuclear movement and the beginnings of the green movement in Europe. Locating the theories in this way makes the rather obvious point that neither theory evolved in any knowledge of the trajectory of social movements in Latin America, or of their role in Latin American politics. The latter part of this chapter therefore examines the relevance of these theories for the study of Latin American social movements, and looks not only at the movements themselves but also at the key dimensions of their political context, including forms of state, regime and civil society. This chapter begins by characterizing the European theory, because this theory most clearly reflects its time and place of origin. The broad brush characterization of this theory (like the subsequent account of resource mobilization theory) is not meant to suggest that all the authors of the school advance exactly the same arguments, but that this is a recognizable corpus of social scientific inquiry.

Global Explanations and Grand Theory

Social movements are often seen as the result of deep changes in the society around them. In this way their explanation depends on 'logically prior' theories of societal transformation (Scott, 1991). The pioneer of this way of thinking was Jurgen Habermas, who saw social movements as a reaction to the increasing rationalization of modern life (Habermas, 1973;

1987). In his view, the 'lifeworld' created within civil society is progressively 'colonized' by the expanding structures of the state and the market economy. A simple interpretation of this process sees private life becoming more politicized by this double encroachment (McAdam et al., 1988). A more nuanced reading notes that Habermas severed the simple correlation of civil society with the private sphere, and argued that both public and private spheres were subject to invasion (Cohen and Arato, 1992). Market pressures can suppress public issues just as bureaucratic rationality can politicize private issues (Assies et al., 1991). Thus, for Habermas social movements arise at the seam between the lifeworld and the system, and express the tension between them.[1] It follows that these movements are usually seen as reactive, defensive and particularistic in outlook. Since feminism makes universal moral and legal claims, in the Enlightenment tradition, Habermas sees it as the only modern movement which is unequivocally on the offensive.

In the same line of argument as Habermas (1973) and O'Connor (1973), Claus Offe (1985; Offe and Wiesenthal, 1985) talks of the difficulty of reconciling capitalism and mass democracy, and the ensuing 'crisis of governability'. Strictly speaking, Offe points to two separate problems. On the one hand, the 'fiscal crisis of the state' diminishes its capacity to legitimate the system overall through its welfare functions; on the other, the growth of corporatism reduces the effective range of democratic mediations between citizen and state (Cohen and Arato, 1992). Both tendencies precipitate the breakdown of political party and trade union apparatuses, and encourage the growth of social movements outside of these institutional constraints. More recently, Scott (1991) has pursued these observations to argue that social movements are a direct result of the 'failure and inadequacies of the institutions of interest intermediation'. Since interest groups and political parties no longer respond to popular demands, social movements arise to press these demands.

The structural changes implicit in the interpretations of Habermas and Offe were condensed by Touraine into the notion of a transition from industrial to post-industrial society (Touraine, 1985b; 1988); while Inglehart (1977) talked of an epochal shift from material to post-material values. Dissatisfaction with the effects of industrialization, frustration with the failing welfare system and new concerns, such as the environment, led to a generalized desire for community, self-realization and personal (rather than professional) satisfaction. Moreover, such values are concentrated in 'new educated classes' which are unable to achieve the income or opportunities that their education led them to expect.

If social movements express the same process of societal change, then they might be expected to have interests and aspirations in common. But they do not. In fact the weight of commentary on social movements emphasizes their diversity rather than their similarity (see Chapter 3), and explains this diversity by the many disparate social conflicts within modern society. Paradoxically, the global explanations of the rise of social movements also predict the end of 'grand theory' (Mills, 1959). For many years social movements remained 'the Cinderella of the social sciences' (Scott, 1991), while functionalism, structuralism and Marxism held sway.[2] But the new age of 'post-isms' has witnessed a striking shift of emphasis from structure to social actor. Recalling Weber, it is now often observed that the complexities of the new reality have outrun the reach of theory.

Alain Touraine has led the way in 'bringing the social actor back in'. He rejects the 'explanation of the actor by the system' and aspires to 'study the production of historical situations by the actors' (Touraine, 1988:10). His post-industrial society is one where, for the first time in history, reflection and action on the foundations of social life become possible. A general capacity for reflection (reflexivity) is manifested in the action of social movements on the alterable, but still structured, relations of civil society (historicity), with the cultural dimensions of this society now assuming central importance (Cohen and Arato, 1992). Touraine's theory has inspired many actor-orientated approaches, including that of the 'cognitive praxis', through which social movements produce their own ideological views and political goals (Eyerman and Jamison, 1991). But the key step was signalled by Touraine himself who recommended a clean break from the 'objectivism' which divorced meaning from consciousness, asserting that the meaning of social movements can only be understood 'through action which is normatively oriented' (Touraine, 1988:11). This Weberian echo goes far to explain the emphasis that this school of social movement theory places on the question of identity.

Social Movements and the Formation of Identities

It was Cohen (1985) who first introduced a distinction between identity-oriented and strategy-oriented approaches to social movements, and Escobar (Escobar and Alvarez, 1992) notes that this distinction is now 'well established'. Cohen was responding to the absence of any sense of strategic interaction in Touraine's argument; and the European school of social movement research has come to focus on identity as the first step in explaining strategic decisions. Without an understanding of identity, of the 'passion of the actors' (Cohen and Arato, 1992), there is no way of explaining *why* social movements move. Moreover, without knowing the values of social actors, it is impossible 'to explain why certain stakes and not others become issues' (Scott, 1991). But if some element of hermeneutic inquiry is essential to the study of social movements, Cohen warns that this should not be 'methodologically absolutized' (Cohen and Arato, 1992:494): social movements must also be seen in interaction with their institutional environment.[3]

Identity has proved to be a slippery concept. Individual actors must come together to form collective identities, but why do they get involved in the first place? Hirschman's answer invokes a Habermasian sense of increasing discontent with consumerism and the spreading scope of rational calculation. Collective action responds to disaffection with both public and private (especially family) life, and offers an opportunity to suspend the narrowly instrumental attitudes which govern most action. In this way, social movements can be understood as a search for solidary values, primary relations and community (Hirschman, 1982). Like clubs and voluntary associations of all kinds, they provide friendship and a sense of belonging. Unlike families, entrance and exit are untrammelled by legal and moral constrictions.

But social actors are already 'embedded' in usually loose social networks, 'especially those based on nationality, race-ethnicity, class, gender or religion' (Mueller, 1992), and these networks encourage identity formation. All such identities finally define who is in and who is out, and social pressure within the network is sufficient to create the kind of 'partial solidarities' which underpin collective action (Tilly et al., 1975). Such identities are never perfected or fixed, but rather express a relatively fragile social composition. Social movements may appear coherent to governments, but 'seen from the bottom up, they are usually much more fragmented and heterogeneous: shifting factions, temporary alliances, diverse interests, a continuous flux of members and hangers on' (Tilly, 1984:310). In time the identity may find organization, rules and leadership, but 'in less institutionalized forms of action its character is closer to a process which must be continually activated to make the action possible' (Melucci, 1988).

This process of 'activating' identity requires a continual engagement in 'the production of meaning' in order to provide a cognitive basis for collective action (McAdam et al., 1988). In other words, a social movement is always reforming its ideological profile in order to encompass the aspirations of its potential supporters. This 'signifying work' of social movements occurs through a 'frame alignment process' (Snow et al., 1986) which can be more or less successful in adjusting reality. By telling the story in the right way, the movement can give all its supporters a part in their own movie. But far from being a contemplative or academic activity, the story advances through struggle, which is always a struggle over meaning as well as resources. 'New frames of meaning result from the struggles within social movements and from their clash with their opponents' (Tarrow, 1992:197). Since the social networks underpinning identity often provide the 'cultural materials' which are used to interpret 'grievances, resources and opportunities' (Mueller, 1992), the cognitive and contextual approaches to collective identity remain broadly compatible.

If these are the processes of identity formation it is no surprise that social movements are seen to project a plurality of struggles which display a broad diversity of aims and ideologies. Indeed, in the radical formulation of Laclau and Mouffe (1985), the political practices of social movements construct the 'interests' they represent. Hence no social struggle is more 'real' or 'central' than any other, and no appeal to structural or 'objective' interests can predict the outcome of such struggles. (The working class, in particular, is not the privileged subject of socialism.) Thus, in this 'decentred' view, identity is a purely discursive product and the choice of values it articulates is completely contingent. This is its weakness, for Laclau and Mouffe have no way of constructing either the context of collective action in general, or the institutional environment of social movements in particular. 'Historical conditions' have disappeared from the picture, so while they may be successful in characterizing the internal development of social movements in terms of the 'discursive constitution of subject positions' (Laclau and Mouffe, 1985:168), the relationship of the social movement with the political world remains opaque.

The New Social Movements Debate

In Touraine's view, the transition from industrial to post-industrial society creates a new 'societal type' (Cohen and Arato, 1992:518) where the identity of social actors corresponds to their capacity for self-reflection or reflexivity. Industrial society saw conflicts over distribution. Post-industrial or 'programmed' society spawns cultural conflicts over historicity, which is society's capacity to produce itself. In this perspective, social movements reflect a qualitative shift in the nature of capitalist society, and are symptoms of change in the 'boundary conditions of the social system'

(Scott, 1991:7). Since this society is 'new', then the social movements themselves are necessarily new.

This 'new social movements' approach emerged from the post-structuralist and post-Marxist trends of the 1970s. The social democratic consensus in post-war Europe had favoured both the construction of the welfare state and the emergence of a strongly 'corporatized' labour movement which played an important role in economic and social policy-making. By comparison with the deeply institutional character of this 'movement' the more recent movements did indeed look new. In the United States, on the other hand, where social democracy was weak and the labour movement much less important, the 'new social movements' debate lacked relevance and so failed to reverberate. The centrality of the labour movement to European politics also goes some way to explain the European emphasis on the diversity of struggles among the new movements: 'the generalization of conflicts deprives them of a concrete central locus' (Touraine, 1988).

The 'new social movements' school is 'actually too various to be represented by a single tendency' (Tarrow, 1988a), and includes German (Claus Offe), French (Alain Touraine) and Italian (Alberto Melucci) versions. But all versions agree that the new movements arise in the period from the 1960s to the present. Tilly agrees that 'the recognition of the historical specificity of the forms of collective action is the beginning of wisdom' (Tilly, 1984:305), but he sees the key change occurring in the nineteenth-century shift from defensive actions by traditional or communal groups to the 'offensive pursuit of new rights and advantages' by organized, self-conscious and sustained movements. Indeed, for Tilly, both the concept and phenomenon of social movement are largely nineteenth-century creations. [4]

Tilly's intention is to reconstruct the impact of this shift from local to national structures of power on the organizational forms and types of collective action. The changing conditions of the nineteenth century created new opportunities for movements to form and mount challenges to the authorities, and with this came a radical transformation of their 'action repertoire'. For Tilly, all forms of collective action are learned forms, and the new ones included mass meetings, strikes, demonstrations, electoral rallies and so forth. New forms were invented, old ones abandoned or adapted. Moreover, this nineteenth century repertoire is still with us today. In comparison with those changes 'the twentieth century's innovations ... look small' (Tilly, 1984:310).

In response to Tilly's explanation of the rise of modern social movements, others have argued that the change from communal and reactive struggles to national and proactive movements may be far from complete. Lo (1992) suggests that many contemporary movements are also rooted in communities, even if these communities are not so production-oriented as in the past. Examples range from the civil rights movement, to the Ku Klux Klan, to various forms of tax protest, to the student movements of Berkeley and Madison. In short, the long transformation of petty capitalism to post-industrial society leaves many residues, and a sense of community continues to be important to popular struggles.

Lo's observations impinge on other aspects of the 'new social movements' debate, and especially the question of identity formation. Touraine (1988) tends to see the cultural emphasis in the new movements as specific to post-industrial society, while Melucci (1989) sees these movements as very different from nineteenth-century movements with their clear class identity and sense of historical direction. But the task of creating identity and solidarity is common to all collective action at all times, and the class identities of the nineteenth century were probably as difficult to construct as contemporary identities of other kinds. Lo insists that many struggles of the new industrial age were rooted in community, and that the idea of class was slowly constructed out of community. These are insights that owe much to E.P. Thompson's classic account of the making of the English working class (Thompson, 1974), besides resonating with the realities of contemporary Latin America, where many movements, both rural and urban, are rooted in forms of community.[5]

Resource Mobilization Theory

The theory of 'new social movements' refers their rise to the new constituencies, values and forms of action created by structural changes in modern society. They are new responses to new grievances. But this focus on structural preconditions diverts attention away from the political problems of mobilization, organization and strategic decision-making. In sum, by insisting on *why* social actors mobilize, the theory ignores the equally important question of *how* they mobilize. Both Touraine and Castells fail to theorize the role of organizations in social mobilization, which is never imagined as a purposive and deliberate process; while Laclau and Mouffe detach their social actors from the institutional contexts which must constrain collective action.

Resource mobilization theory, on the contrary, begins with the premise that social discontent is universal but collective action is not. It is inherently difficult to organize a social movement, and the main problem is mobilizing sufficient resources to maintain and expand the movement. Hence, in its simplest formulation, 'resource mobilization is based on the idea that successful movements acquire resources and create advantageous exchange relationships with other groups as they achieve success in fulfilling their goals' (Costain, 1992:xiv). Organization and leadership are necessary precisely because the movement is goal-oriented and must make the strategic choices that may achieve those goals.[6]

In its initial statements, resource mobilization theory preceded the European notion of 'new social movements', emerging as a response to functionalist accounts of the irrational and unorganized nature of collective action. It replaced the crowd with the organization, and dismissed the psychological variables of alienation and frustration in favour of the rational actor employing instrumental and strategic reasoning. But the original and strictly utilitarian logic of rational choice, pioneered by Olson (1965), made collective action unlikely because of the now famous 'free rider' problem. According to Olson, this action cannot flow naturally from the rational pursuit of shared interests because the average group member's estimated return from joining in the action will be less than the cost of so doing. Moreover, in the world of social movements the long-term and uncertain benefits of social mobilization and change have to be weighed against both the costs of participation and the short-term benefits of adhering to the status quo. Hence, collective action can only occur if the 'free rider' problem is overcome through selective incentives or sanctions.

Resource mobilization theory has developed in many directions since Olson's statement, and it is now accepted that solidary and purposive incentives are just as important as selective ones, and that the structural location of the individual is critical to the moment of 'choice'.[7] In addition, the theory has expanded its explanatory power by including a range of ancillary arguments. First, dense social networks make mobilization more likely. Secondly, more prosperity favours social mobilization by facilitating resource mobilization in different ways. Finally, levels of prior social organization influence the degree and type of social mobilization. These arguments might plausibly be applied as much to college campuses or the civil rights movement in the United States as to urban neighbourhoods and urban social movements in Latin America. But it is fair to say that the theory has been comprehensively ignored in most research on social movements in Latin America, and this has hindered a proper understanding of their organizational constraints and political possibilities.

Critiques of the Resource Mobilization Approach

It is a measure of resource mobilization theory's importance that its critiques occupy much of the theoretical literature on social movements. These critiques focus on the theory's adherence to economic models of human agency, or what is often called 'methodological individualism'. This creates two main problems. First, social actors are presumed to employ a narrowly instrumental rationality which bridges a rigid means/end distinction. The careful weighing of costs and benefits implied by the means/end model falls far short of a universal or complete account of collective action, if only because action 'may be its own reward' (Hirschman, 1982). More particularly, to recall Weber's analysis of social action, the motives that predispose the actor to act may be not merely instrumental, but habitual, affective and, above all, expressive. Secondly, social actors are presumed to exercise this rationality without reference to their social context. They may be 'efficient and often even ingenious and devious' but they are 'without a history' (Hirschman, 1982). With no sense of context it is impossible to see how the actor's preferences are formed, or how costs and benefits are calculated. And this sets the theory a tautological trap, for it must then define the actor's interests in such a way that no matter what choice is made it is always seen to further those interests. [8]

On both counts the critiques make clear that an adequate account of social movements must include 'the cultural as well as the purposive aspects' (Scott, 1991:111) of their activity. Otherwise it might easily be forgotten that the concepts of resource mobilization theory do not refer to 'objective' realities but to the capacity of social actors to perceive and evaluate the limits and opportunities of the environment, and that this capacity depends in turn on the construction of a collective identity (Melucci, 1988). In short, 'any strategic paradigm necessarily supposes a theory of identity' (Gamson, 1992), because 'collective action is never based solely on cost-benefit calculation, and a collective identity is never entirely negotiable' (Melucci, 1988:343). Without these cultural considerations it is 'difficult to see how solidary action would be possible' (Scott, 1991), and the critical consensus is that social movements occur much more often than resource mobilization theory can properly explain. In particular, it fails to explain social movements that are too weak to distribute selective benefits, and tends to ignore movements which go unrecognized by government authorities.

Further objections to the theory tend to turn on its static presentation of strategic choice. Since such choice is often a result of interaction with a living political environment, it makes little sense to think of it as uncontaminated by negotiation, 'and the more negotiation that is involved in the development of strategies, the harder the task of their analysis becomes' (Crow, 1989:14). Moreover, the rationality applying to one-off game-like situations does not necessarily apply to long-term relationships (Lash and Urry, 1984:37). At the same time the 'interests' or preferences which inform the choice may change in at least two ways. On the one hand, social actors can 'alter' the high costs of collective action by 'changing the standards according to which these costs are subjectively estimated within their own collectivity' (Offe and Wiesenthal, 1985). On the other, the very process of organization and mobilization may modify the interests which gave rise to them in the first place, so that actual interests may even come to conflict with the original (Michels, 1949). These latter points are complicated by the relationship between leaders and led and the so-called 'iron law of oligarchy', because the theory tends to assume that 'goals, ideology and strategy are determined by the leadership while the membership is treated as a resource' (Hannigan, 1985:441).

The Political Process Approach

In recent years social movement theorists have attempted either to repair and extend resource mobilization theory or to achieve some form of synthesis between the 'new social movements' and resource mobilization approaches. On the one hand was a European literature which looked at the structural origins of social movements without analysing the political conditions which facilitated or hindered collective action. Politics was reduced to a residual category or to a transmission belt (e.g. Castells, 1983; Touraine, 1985a). On the other was a North American literature which insisted on the political questions of organization and strategy without analysing either social context or political context in the form of the state. Reviewing these literatures, Tarrow discerned a conceptual convergence around the problems of 'connecting collective action to politics' (Tarrow, 1988a:428), and this he called the 'political process model'.

Historical research had shown the need to bring the state back into the analysis. Although Tilly had focused on social conflicts within civil society, he clearly saw these as offensive or defensive reactions to changing power relations at regional and national levels (Tilly, 1978; 1984; 1985). Then, with the development of national politics during the nineteenth century, it became evident that social movements vary in character and organization with the kinds of political authority they challenge. Where the 'action repertoire' of social movements changed, it was prima facie evidence of a change in the 'structure of power'. In short, the collective identity and strategic intent of social movements remains indeterminate until they are analysed in interaction with the political environment, and especially with the institutions of the state. Social movements were no longer unstructured collective action, but a form of mass politics. It also became apparent that rational choice assumptions became quite inappropriate in highly unequal power relationships.[9]

Once the state was back in the picture it was also possible to introduce the notion of a 'political opportunity structure' (Klandermans et al., 1988) composed of state institutions and national political traditions. This structure conditioned the emergence, strategy and likelihood of success of social movements; and by extending the analysis to supportive third parties and political allies it brought the study of social movements closer to traditional political science. At the same time, the question of values or 'interests' now encompassed state and social movement, because the 'multiple reactions' provoked by social mobilization depended 'as much on the values of the agents of the state as on the logic of its particular way of working' (Birnbaum, 1988:54). The analytical result of these additions to the theory would depend on their application. They could lead to the simple conclusion that 'when government is strong and committed to repressing a social movement, the movement will usually fail' (Costain, 1992:xv). Or they could lead to a complex research programme into the 'social and political terrain that forms the condition of possibility for the emergence and success of modern movements' (Cohen and Arato, 1992:499).

Linking Micro *and* Macro *Approaches*

Just as resource mobilization theory came to recognize the importance of the state in the political process model, so it began to address the roots of civil society in the idea of the 'micro mobilization context'. Another general review of social movement theory (McAdam et al., 1988) concluded that there was a large gap in our understanding of social mobilization. On the one hand was a range of theories,[10] including rational choice theory, which purported to explain this mobilization at the level of individual participation. On the other was the political process model which provided analysis of political conditions and context. Therefore the main problem with the whole field was that it left 'the links between the macro and micro levels of analysis unexamined'. This gap led to a recurrent incoherence in the theory, whenever it was unclear whether it was focused on individual or collective actors.

McAdam, McCarthy and Zald (1988) proposed to marry the micro and macro perspectives by focusing on the micromobilization context which connected 'private troubles to public issues' (Mills, 1959) by providing a 'structure of solidary incentives' to aggregate individual choices into programmes of action. This 'cell structure of collective action' worked to concentrate resources such as communication and leadership, as well as creating the 'rudiments of organization' (McAdam et al., 1988:711). Examples of such cells would be union branches, groups within unions, black churches (USA), mosques (Iran), Catholic base communities (Latin America) and personal networks of all kinds. Structural changes or 'macro' processes such as urbanization, migration, or the mass entry of women into the job market would create more or less propitious conditions for cell growth and reproduction.

The micromobilization context recalls the social networks which underpin 'identity' and suggests further convergence between European and North American approaches. Melucci too had noticed the gap between structural determinants and individual preferences, and had called for more analysis of 'an intermediate level' where individuals 'recognize what they have in common and decide to act together' (Melucci, 1988:339). Melucci continued to focus on the question of identity, but his 'social movements sectors' (or indeed Klandermans' 'recruitment networks') have much in common with McAdam's micromobilization context, and both contribute equally to mute instrumental attitudes to mobilization and so mitigate the free-rider problem.

The upshot of these efforts is simply that individual and group must enter the analysis simultaneously. 'Without individuals there is nobody to share with and without collective beliefs there is nothing to share' (Klandermans, 1992). In this way the individual motivation to participate 'cannot be considered as an exclusively individual variable' (Melucci, 1988:339) because all potential participants are 'rational actors embedded in networks'. Hence, 'most movements do not arise because isolated individuals choose to join the struggle. Rather, established groups redefine group membership to include commitment to the movement as one of its obligations' (Friedman and McAdam, 1992:163).[11]

Synthesizing the Identity *and* Strategy *Approaches*

A mainly European insistence on identity tends to confine social movements to civil society, while the mainly North American focus on strategy places them in political society (see Chapter 1). The first approach accounts for actors' preferences and the process of identity formation. Logically, it should also explore the interaction of social movements with other social actors within civil society, but this topic has not received any sustained attention in the literature. The second explains how social movements define their aims and achieve their political effects (Scott, 1991:133). Its primary point of reference is therefore the state (and this makes resource mobilization theory potentially very useful in analysing the trajectory of Latin American movements, as Chapter 4 will show). But despite these crucial differences the two approaches see social movements in essentially the same way. Both assume that these movements 'are based on conflicts between organized groups ... with sophisticated forms of communication ... and both argue that conflictual collective action is normal and that participants are usually rational, well-integrated members of organizations' (Cohen and Arato, 1992:497). Hence it may be possible to construct a synthesis of the two approaches that treats social movements as both expressive and instrumental, as both resource generators and resource mobilizers (Cohen, 1985).

Jean Cohen has recently reconstructed social movement theory in order to provide just such a synthesis. She argues that the two approaches work with different logics of collective action, but that they are not incompatible. Indeed, any single social movement can involve both the construction of personal and collective identity ('communicative' creation in Habermas' language) and instrumental and strategic activity. It may struggle both for the defence and democratization of civil society and for inclusion within and the expansion of political society. Within this 'dual logic' or 'dualistic character of contemporary collective action' (Cohen and Arato, 1992:508) the civil rights movement (in the United States) sought both civil rights and the removal of traditional norms of social control, while the feminist movement aspires to change patriarchal institutions as well as winning economic and political power. In short, these modern movements have 'civil society as both *target* and *terrain* of collective action' (author's emphasis, Cohen and Arato, 1922:509).

Cohen's synthesis is rooted in a re-reading of Habermas, who saw modern social movements as universally defensive, in the sense of defending their patch of the 'lifeworld'.[12] In her view, Habermas underestimated the potential of associationalism, which not only fosters new identities but also generates conflict over social relations within civil institutions. In this connection 'defensive' movements can promote institutional change within civil society, while 'offensive' movements will seek insertion in political society. But it is axiomatic in Cohen that most movements will be both defensive and offensive, and that civil society can and will influence processes of political and economic change.

Cohen rejects any interpretation of the 'dual logic' of social movements as 'stages' in a linear model of development, with the first stage creating identity and the second focusing on strategic action. In that way the shift from expressive to instrumental activity and from informal to formal organization might be 'understood as a learning process involving goal-rational adaptation to political structures' (Cohen and Arato, 1992:557). Michels' 'iron law of oligarchy' might then be invoked to explain that success in institutional terms spells the end of the movement and the dilution of its aims. But Cohen insists that the two logics continue together in time, with many movements succeeding in occupying both civil and political societies simultaneously. In her view the 'stage' model suffers both from an inadequate sense of political learning, implying that the 'politics of identity' cannot be rational, and an impoverished conception of politics in general, implying that civil society cannot influence outcomes in political society. [13]

The rejection of the 'stagist' model requires a new look at the relationship between identity and strategy. Both North American and European approaches to social mobilization see identity as coming first. In resource mobilization theory 'the rational choice model has encouraged ... researchers to see attitudes or preferences as pre-existing and stable structures, logically prior to and predictive of behavior' (Marx Ferree, 1992); while 'new social movements' theorists like Melucci insist that it is the prior construction of identity, of a notion of 'we', which allows social actors to assess costs and benefits, and so to engage in strategic thinking. But if social movements are simultaneously cultural and political it follows that 'preference formation' occurs 'within collective action and not just as an exogenous variable' (Scott, 1991:122). In other words, identity cannot simply be conceived as a precondition of strategic action, because the processes of organization and strategic choice contribute crucially to construct and shape this identity (Foweraker, 1993:176–9).

But care must be taken not to throw the baby out with the bath water. The identity of social movements is neither the direct expression of structurally shaped and knowable 'interests', nor is it created from nothing by organization and strategic activity. The shared experience of structural contradictions and inequalities may still be necessary but not sufficient to explain social mobilization that will also depend on 'a host of other factors which are context specific' (Scott, 1991:53) such as the presence or absence of emotive issues, potential leaders or possible allies, as well as the reaction of the authorities and the outcomes of strategic choices. In short, identity can never be an entirely contingent product of the very process of mobilization, as Laclau and Mouffe (1985) suggest, because social location and shared experience provide its raw materials. But significant contingencies do enter its formation, and not simply because strategic choices often have unexpected outcomes. More critically, strategic choices do not themselves reflect the purpose of a singular rational calculation, but are the highly contingent result of complex series of interactions, both within the movement itself and between the movement and its political environment (Foweraker, 1993:173–6).[14] Consequently the process of identity formation can never be predicted or controlled. The European theory makes much of the 'reflexivity' of modern movements and their preoccupation with identity: Who are we? But there is little sense that the answer may come as a complete surprise.

Social Movements as Social Process

Despite the range of social movement theory, a satisfactory definition of social movements remains elusive. Nonetheless, there is some agreement that the social movement must be defined not as a group of any kind, but as a process. An early definition talked of 'a deliberate collective endeavour to promote change in any direction and by any means, not excluding violence, illegality, revolution or withdrawal into "utopian" community' (Wilkinson, 1971); and, although Scott does refer to a collective actor with a common identity, he again includes the commitment to change (either society itself or the position of the group in society), and asserts that it is the character of 'mass mobilization' as the 'prime source of social sanction' which distinguishes this actor from others such as political parties and pressure groups (Scott, 1991). But it is Charles Tilly who has most insisted that the social movement is 'a sustained interaction between a specific set of authorities and various spokespersons for a given challenge to those authorities' (Tilly, 1984:305).[15]

Although the effervescence of social mobilization has been described as a 'moment of madness' (Tarrow, 1987), for Tilly the longer-term process is characterized by 'action repertoires' or 'repertoires of contention' which are remarkably stable across time, partly because they respond to what people have come to expect, and these expectations change very slowly (see 'The Political Process Approach', above). Setting out to reconcile these contrary images, Tarrow proposed to connect momentary madness to the ages of contention by the 'cycles of protest' that introduce new forms of action into the repertoire. Besides the innovations which are 'diffused, tested and refined into more institutional forms' (Tarrow, 1987:5) the cycle may also modify or extend more conventional forms of protest. Strike activity, for example, may expand to include public demonstrations, or deepen with the organization of workers' councils.

The moments of madness are important to historical development, playing an analogous role to that of 'charisma' in Weber's historical sociology, and triggering the cycles of protest. But in the *longue durée* they 'are soon mere blips on the curve of history' (Tarrow, 1987:21), whereas the cycles last much longer and have a more enduring influence over events. Finally Tarrow adds that this can only be true of democratic or open systems, because under authoritarian regimes the moments of madness are mere interludes in the long saga of repression and demobilization. But here he is wrong, and the evidence of popular struggle under authoritarian regimes in Latin America in recent years tells a quite different story. First, it demonstrates the extraordinary range of tactical and strategic invention which has extended and strengthened the action repertoire of social movements across the continent (Foweraker, 1993). Secondly, it reveals how cycles of protest have characterized the process of social mobilization even in very repressive circumstances (see Chapter 4).

Social Movement Theory and Latin America

Although social movement research may have stimulated social science in some countries of Latin America (Escobar and Alvarez, 1992), there is some doubt whether new social movement theory may be properly applied to the continent. Attempts to do so appear to be 'guided ... by Euro-centred paradigms and plain old wishful thinking' (Davis, 1989:226). It is alleged that 'lowered expectations' and 'disillusion with dreams of the past' have led intellectuals (especially those of more radical bent) to apply the 'new' label to social phenomena that would never have qualified as social movements twenty years ago (Lehmann, 1990b:158). At that time movement meant labour or union movement, with an identifiable membership and a clear institutional context. Nowadays every social or cultural association merits movement status as long as it is 'new' (see Chapter 3). This tendency of the new social movements approach to reify its object of study may also mean that the theory misses important movements that are not 'new' enough in the European sense (Gamson, 1992). Consequently, with some exceptions (Escobar and Alvarez, 1992), the initial enthusiasm for 'new social movements' in Latin America (Mainwaring and Viola, 1984; Slater, 1985; Jelin, 1985) has now subsided. It is now more normal to talk of social movements *tout court* or of popular movements (Foweraker and Craig, 1990).

The main problem is that European theory resonates within its European context, but does not necessarily reflect Latin American realities. One example which recurs frequently in the literature is that of Castells' theory of urban social movements as a response to 'urban contradictions' (Castells, 1983). In this account the social movements are seeking to increase collective consumption, defend community culture and achieve political self-management, with each of these aims addressing specific contradictions that have created specific 'enemies' (the bourgeoisie, the technocracy and the state, respectively) within the urban environment. But Latin American theorists object that Castells' contradictions correspond to new state forms in advanced capitalist countries (Cardoso, 1983), and that his urban movements bear an uncanny resemblance to the counter cultural movements of the 1960s in those countries. Urban movements in Latin America are far too diverse to be classified under Castells' conceptually ambitious categories, which miss the central contradiction between those with stable employment and secure housing, and the massive population living in complete deprivation (Machado and Ziccardi, 1983).

European theories have enjoyed a far greater vogue in Latin America than North American ones, but resource mobilization theory does not escape scepticism about its applicability outside the United States. A feminist critique accuses the theory of ignoring race, class and gender specificities in favour of a 'pseudo-universal human actor', who is none other than a white middle-class male in Western capitalist society (Marx Ferree, 1992). Hence, the 'self-interest' which operates as a general guide to collective action is actually 'grounded in a system where women must be "self-less", non-whites and women should be protected, and other cultures are "primitive" or "backward" because they do not run by these rules' (Marx Ferree, 1992:41). This critique has a certain force in the Latin American context where ethnicity buttresses social inequalities, where women compose the majority of most urban social movements, and where 'class specific concerns and experience obviously still fuel the most visible, and most common forms of protest and resistance' (Davis, 1989:233).

It is further suggested that resource mobilization theory has restricted its purview to movements which pursue middle-class reform goals and eschew open, and especially violent, conflict (Mueller, 1992). Tilly's 'stagist' notion of 'action repertoires' endorses a division between the violence of pre- or early industrial protest and the more peaceful programmes of modern times. Rights are granted, the costs of collective action diminish, and all that comes to matter is the 'group's capacity to organize, accumulate resources and form alliances' (Piven and Cloward, 1992). Once it is assumed that ordinary people are able to pursue their goals through 'normal politics' the theory comes close to the idea of a generic social movement, always motivated by the same kind of grievance, always seeking a similar degree of change.

If this conclusion appears inappropriate in the United States, it is plainly inadequate in Latin America where vast disparities of income and opportunity raise the stakes of social conflict, and where authoritarian regimes and state repression have often made 'normal politics' impossible. But this does not warrant rejection of the whole theory. The resource mobilization approach may not easily encompass violent conflict and armed confrontation, but most social movements in Latin America are not violent; rather they pursue institutional advance through careful strategic calculation (see Chapter 4). Military and revolutionary movements such as the FSLN, the FMLN and *Sendero Luminoso* comprise a tiny minority of social movements across the continent, even if they are highly visible; and even their activities include the search for political allies and the calculation of political opportunities. Indeed, tactical and strategic questions clearly become acute in conditions where they decide immediate physical survival. Finally, to exclude resource mobilization theory from Latin America because 'the crucial resources ... are lacking' (Schuurman, 1989:15) is to stand reality on its head: the central importance of the state as the dispenser of scarce resources means that social movements in Latin America must develop a strategic approach to the state; and this suggests that resource mobilization theory can be useful in analysing the political trajectory of these movements.

Similarities Between Social Movements in Europe and Latin America

Despite the scepticism surrounding the application of European and North American theory to Latin America, it is not difficult to discern some similarities between social movements in Europe and Latin America. The common characteristics are said to include a concern with basist democracy, an independence from established political parties, and a rejection of traditional institutional politics. Moreover movements in both places are now supposed to address cultural concerns, and to emphasize the kind of expressive and symbolic politics that connects personal lifestyles to political change. Thus when Touraine argues that 'private life is more than ever a public thing, the stake of a social movement, the central theme of emergent social conflicts' (Touraine, 1988:14), he recalls the authoritarian invasion of private space by the military regimes of Latin America's southern cone (Oszlak, 1987); and his axiomatic statement that 'we simply claim our freedom, the right to be ourselves without being crushed by the apparatuses of power, violence and propaganda' (Touraine, 1988:18) reverberates with the popular struggle for democracy in that continent (see Chapter 5). Indeed, the large and centralized management apparatuses which Touraine sees as specific to post-industrial society are analogous in some degree to the unwieldy 'technobureaucracy' which advanced state control of economy and society under the 'national security' regimes of the 1970s and 1980s; while the democratic struggle precipitated 'cycles of protest' against those regimes (O'Donnell and Schmitter, 1986) that closely resemble the Italian experience (Tarrow, 1991).

Yet the unequivocally 'new' social movements in Latin America are few and far between (see Chapter 3). The ecology movement has emerged from nothing, especially in Brazil where the destruction of the Amazon rain forest has spurred its growth; the human rights movement has played a key role in the fight against military regimes, especially in Argentina and Chile; and the women's movement has expanded rapidly throughout the continent and raised a range of new issues such as 'domestic violence, economic dependence, sexual aggression, discrimination in the workplace, lack of reproductive control, and clandestine abortion' (Jaquette, 1989:172). But the real degree of overlap between new social movements in Europe and Latin America remains limited. In itself this is no impediment to comparative work, if the analytical arguments can be made to stick. Scott's argument that the growth of social movements in Europe is the result of a general failure of 'interest inter-mediation' by traditional political institutions and actors (Scott, 1991) appears congruent with the rise of these movements under authoritarian regimes in Latin America and their relative decline during democratic transition and consolidation (see Chapter 5). The key question then becomes whether the huge differences in historical context and political culture inevitably vitiate any comparisons that might be drawn.

*Contextual Differences Between Europe, the United States
and Latin America*

Social movements in Europe and North America arose under different forms of liberal democratic regime during a period of social
democratic consensus (which was stronger in Europe than the
United States). The policy patterns of Keynesianism and Fordism
had created a broadly-based 'societal' corporatism (Schmitter,
1974) linked to welfare programmes which provided collective
means of consumption and protected labour from the worst
excesses of capital. Above all, these movements emerged within a
dense and communicative civil society, meaning 'public spaces,
social institutions (mass media, the press), rights (to associate, to
speak, to assemble), representative political institutions, and an
autonomous legal system' (Cohen and Arato, 1992:497). All these
civil and political institutions are legitimate 'targets for social movements seeking to influence policy or initiate change'. In fact, Cohen
is clear that 'collective action involves forms of association and
strategies specific to the context of a modern pluralist civil society',
for these are the foundations for a 'politics of influence' which is
'the key element missing in most paradigms used for the study of
social movements today' (Cohen and Arato, 1992:560).[16] But this
'politics of influence' (rather than 'of power' or 'of inclusion')
appears to presuppose the civil and political conditions of North
America or Europe. What of social movements that have grown
from a very different soil?

In sharp contrast to Europe and North America, social movements in Latin America have mainly emerged under authoritarian
and military regimes. The majority of these regimes founded or
developed different forms of state corporatism (Schmitter, 1974;
Foweraker, 1987) which both advanced labour control and
restricted the reach of welfarism. Consequently their 'formal rep-
resentational political structures often embodied social or class
interests in ways unparalleled in the democratic systems of
advanced capitalist nations' (Davis, 1989:227). Crucially, the
movements arose within weak and deliberately divided civil societies, which might themselves suffer from strong authoritarian
tendencies. (The military dictatorship in Argentina encouraged
and succoured many 'micro despotisms' within the family, the
school, the factory and the college, with many Argentines acting
as willing *kapos* of the regime (O'Donnell, 1984).) The weak
welfarist tradition led Latin American movements to struggle to
secure basic social services and public utilities. The authoritarianism made basic civil liberties and the rights of citizenship their
central concern. In the 'North' these were 'old' demands. But that

is the point. 'Northern' theory could take as 'its starting point and object of criticism a liberal democracy which is precisely one of the major objectives of South American movements' (Mainwaring and Viola, 1984).

In Europe the grand theory had seen social movements as responses to the secular processes implicit in Habermas' account of the colonization of the lifeworld, namely increasing commodification, bureaucratization and massification. In Latin America it is rather the acute centralization of power and decision-making in the state that has catalysed the process of social mobilization. Public administration, in particular, has concentrated an increasing number of productive and regulatory agencies which have intensified state interference in economic and social life, so that 'struggles over employment concerns and production issues are as frequently waged between subordinate classes and the state as between dominant and subordinate classes' (Davis, 1989:227). And more than the massive expansion of the state in Mexico (Cornelius and Craig, 1984) or the 'pervasiveness of the state' in Brazil (Boschi, 1987), what matters is that Latin America's social movements arose 'while institution building took place in the political system as a whole' (Boschi, 1987:201). Thus it is the state which has become the main focus for social movements in Latin America, despite disenchantment with populist politics, the crisis of the traditional left and the adverse political climate of the authoritarian regimes.

Civil society can never be independent of the state in the majority of countries 'whose societies are dominated by the voluntarist action of the State rather than by class conflicts' (Touraine, 1988:157), and in Latin America even the idea of civil society often had to be rescued from an authoritarian, modernizing and 'monstrous' state (Weffort, 1984:1989). As Weffort suggested, if civil society did not exist, it had to be invented; if it was small, it had to be made to grow. Civil society was necessary because freedom was desirable, and this gave social movements a special importance. Their scope may merely be local, sectoral or, at the most, regional (Slater, 1991).[17] Even then 'the actual reach of social movements (may be) exaggerated, particularly with respect to other social segments, including labor and political parties' (Boschi, 1987a:183). But social movements in Latin America have had a symbolic and political importance in recovering civil society as a 'space of freedom' (Scherer-Warren and Krischke, 1987) which is more than the sum of specific struggles in particular places.

But recuperating civil society in Latin America is a deeply contradictory process, because the formation of social identities is so deeply influenced by the state. On the one hand, primary class identities 'are more complex and fluid' (Davis, 1989:226) and collective action in the continent tends to have a multiclass basis. This is as true of the neighbourhood associations in big cities as it is of the cross-class alliances which sustained popular resistance to authoritarian rule in Chile or Brazil. On the other, this fluidity does not represent 'an inevitable turn to new social identities associated with commodification, bureaucratization and massifica-tion' (Davis, 1989), but, more simply, a new kind of identity forged in interaction or confrontation with the state. Interaction is seen in neighbourhood associations, promoted by populist politicians, which yet develop their own impetus; while confronta-tion is seen in the 'conscious and necessary strategy' (Davis, 1989) of mass or multiclass opposition to authoritarian and repressive regimes. In short, the identity of social movements in Latin America is not so much formed through social relations as it is 'constituted at the political level' (Moises, 1981), and the recovery of civil society therefore occurs in intimate interrelation with the state.

The political level is composed of the party system, where it exists, and clientelism, corporatism and state-civil society relations in general. Recent studies on Mexico show how corporatist struc-tures 'give both organization and incentive for grassroots mobili-zation, even when changing those structures is the goal' (Davis, 1992:402; Foweraker and Craig, 1990). But Mexico was excep-tional in the extent to which popular sectors 'were encouraged and able to participate politically, despite the absence of formal democracy' (Davis, 1992: 402) and, in most cases, the construc-tion of new identities also corresponded to an intensive search for new forms of political organization and for effective political strategies (Foweraker, 1989a:1993). This often led to a gradual rejection of state-sanctioned and state-chartered divisions between production and reproduction, the public and the private, the world of work and the world of recreation. In the ways suggested by social movement theory, new sociabilities and solidarities began to underpin the new identities (Scherer-Warren and Krischke, 1987:62) which began to form through collective action itself. One powerful example (which will recur throughout the argument) is the emergence of women as the majority presence in collective action on the urban periphery. Thus social movements were formed in interaction with the authoritarian state, but the state did not therefore determine their root identities. Possibly the 'newness' of social movements in Latin America (see Chapter 3) lay in the introduction of popular and previously excluded sectors into the balance of forces within civil society, and in their occasional ability to challenge the state (Cardoso, 1983:224).[18]

Social Movements and the Latin American State

In this way the overwhelming presence of the state in the political economies of Latin America has created a specific political and cultural context for social movement activity. It is clearly different from the context that supports most social movement theory. The theory sees social movements as occupying and expanding a 'public sphere' within civil society (Habermas, 1989). By bringing new issues and values into this sphere, the movements help to reproduce the consensus that pluralist democratic theory presupposes but often fails to explain (Cohen and Arato, 1992:19). In Latin America this public space has been lacking, or is far more restricted, with the state a bulwark of social and economic exclusion. Hence social movements have mainly sought local and immediate solutions to concrete problems. The 'movement' then refers to the dissemination of demands by an accumulation of similar groups, and not to the unified phenomenon imagined by Touraine (1988). Even where coordinating and umbrella organizations have emerged, as in Brazil and Mexico, they 'often prove feeble and discontinuous' (Assies et al., 1991:102).

The theory suggests that social movements respond to a post-industrial society of 'symbolic goods' (Assies et al., 1991:104) and that they project post-material values such as anticonsumerism. If they have a defined social base, it is among the educated middle classes who have the time and income to organize and agitate. But the basic issue for most communities and associations in Latin America remains how to consume enough to survive, and material demands remain paramount for the great majority of social movements. It is mainly the lower or 'popular' classes which mobilize for reasons of work, wages, services and housing. This exacerbates the dispersion of the movements around specific demands for land titles, water supplies, bus transport, health posts, etc., but it also concentrates these demands in the state as provider of public services and guarantor of the conditions of collective consumption.

The problem is that the state is generally incapable of carrying out these tasks in an efficient or effective fashion. In Chile this was a result of the military regime's deliberate deindustrialization and its rejection of any responsibility for welfare. In authoritarian Brazil, very differently, the ambitious economic and social goals of the 'developmentalist' state were continually subverted by the kind of corruption and clientelism that catalysed social mobilization. In both cases, however, and elsewhere, social movements had inherited the ambiguous legacy of the preceding period of populist politics which had conceded a limited or 'corporate'

range of rights to subordinate social groups (see Chapter 5) at
the cost of their dependent integration into the political system.
The divisive effects of populism aggravated the structural segmen-
tation typical of dependent industrial development to create the
'heterogeneous' (Moises et al., 1977) or 'fragmented' (Calderon
and Jelin, 1987) popular classes who turned to the state for social
succour or political redress. Therefore the state's failure or refusal
to fulfil these roles might always act as a spur to social movements.

In this context, urban social movements proliferated, and
became the principal focus of social movement research (Davis,
1992:401; Boschi, 1987b). On the one hand, the urban environment was becoming more important as a result of a dramatic shift
in the demographic structure of the continent. Brazil was already
a predominantly urban country in 1970, but just a decade later
over 75 per cent of its population lived in cities of more than
100,000 people. On the other, the state had become ever more
involved both in controlling the urban poor (Machado and Ziccardi, 1983) and in exploiting them through the pricing of housing, utilities and services (Nunes and Jacobi, 1983; Kowarick,
1982). The expansion of squatter settlements and spontaneous
colonization on the urban peripheries of Chile, Peru and Mexico
had created a new generation of 'militant metropolitan dwellers'
since the 1960s (Castells, 1982:250), while eight thousand neighbourhood associations across Brazil made social movements 'a
key element in the dynamics of social change' in that country
(Boschi, 1987a:180).

Thus urban social movements are not merely a natural result
of poverty or 'marginality' but a response to state policies.[19]
Women are in the majority in most urban movements, and the
policies do much to shape their demands. In the United States
and Europe women tend to seek gender-neutral participation in
the public sphere, but in Latin America it is their roles as
wives and mothers which motivate and legitimate their social
protest and political participation (Sternbach et al., 1992; Safa,
1990). They mobilize around the rising cost of living or declining social services in order to protect and promote the integrity
of children and the family. In short, since it is private nurturing
that leads to collective action, women's mobilization can occur
without feminist conviction. At the same time this 'peripheral
state' is 'more reliant on the family and the private sphere' both
for welfare provision and for assuring social stability (Alvarez,
1990). This made it more impervious to women's claims, and
led the military regimes of recent decades to impose severe
restrictions on the scope of women's political activity.

Their primary identity as wives and mothers led women to

seek greater political participation in social movements, labour unions, and even political parties in their attempt to make the state more responsive to their needs (Safa, 1990). This was fiercely resisted by the military regimes which used terror and torture to drive women back into the domestic environment. The repressive and obsessive practices of torture-rape, child torture and child theft (with children given to military families) has been seen as a gendered response to women's mobilization – a frightening assertion of masculine power (Franco, 1992).[20] This paradoxical project of defending the family by violating its sanctity clearly contributed to politicize women, endowing the concept of 'the personal is political' with a 'very special meaning' in the Latin American context (Jaquette, 1989:205). For this reason the women's movement in Latin America 'is closely linked to human rights ... and is anti-authoritarian' (Jaquette, 1989:205). In sum, its agendas and strategies are likely to be quite distinct from those of the women's movements in Europe and North America.

Social Movement Theory and Latin America Revisited

This quick overview of some of the more salient Latin American social movements suggests that even those that are certainly new are likely to be different from the new social movements in Europe or North America. Some social movement theorists accept this difference and offer their own theoretical explanations for it. Laclau and Mouffe argue that the plural social movements in central capitalist countries represent authentic, if diverse, democratic struggles, whereas the social movements of Latin America are uniformly popular struggles surrounding a central political core of despotism and imperialism (Laclau and Mouffe, 1985). But even if the state in Latin America constitutes a clear political 'centre' (and there is some truth in this), the evidence does not support an equally clear unity of popular identities or popular purpose (see Chapter 3). Similarly Touraine argues that 'pure' social movements engaged in struggles over 'historicity' can only be found in the democracies of central capitalism, and that the stake for Latin American movements 'is not historicity but participation in the political system' (Escobar and Alvarez, 1992:71). Conditions of economic dependency and the broad scope of state intervention into all aspects of social life in Latin America mean that there are no social movements proper, but only 'historical movements' (Touraine, 1989), but this distinction depends on Touraine's original definition of a social movement as challenging society's basic rules and seeking no place in the existing political system (Touraine, 1988).

Social movements in the capitalist centre and in Latin America may be different political animals, but this is no reason to deny the Latin American movements' equal status by definitional fiat. This would make little sense in a world where social movements at the centre have been growing weaker since the 1960s (Touraine, 1988; 1989), whereas in Latin America and Eastern Europe (not to mention Poland, China or South Africa) 'movements have tended to be far more global and comprehensive than in the West' (Cohen and Arato, 1992:81). Nor, finally, are differences of political context or content between 'central' and Latin American movements sufficient to disqualify the application of social movement theory to Latin America. Social movements may be specific responses to specific changes in the surrounding society and polity but they are all forms of collective action, and are all equally available for theories of social agency.

There is no doubt that large structural and contextual changes such as the decline of import-substitution industrialization, the collapse of the populist compromise or the advent of military authoritarianism have influenced the formation and trajectory of social movements in Latin America.[21] But the ideological, organizational and institutional components of collective action are just as important in explaining the rise of social movements across the continent during the 1970s and 1980s (Slater, 1991). Hence, identity-oriented theories certainly have a role to play in exploring the social networks and communities which underpin urban social movements, or Christian base communities and the role of the progressive church, or the formation of new identities among women and indigenous groups in Latin America (see Chapter 3); while the expansion of social demands and the massive presence of the state sharpens the relevance of the relationship of social movements to their political environment, and makes the questions of organization, strategy and resources essential to their analysis (see Chapter 4). Finally, the fact that most modern social movements of Latin America have arisen under authoritarian rather than liberal democratic regimes makes them more rather than less important to democracy and democratic theory, and theories of civil society and the 'dual logic' of social movements bear directly on the role and fate of these movements in recent 'transitions to democracy' in the continent (see Chapter 5).

Social movement theory has interpreted social movement activity in a specific historical context which includes material plenty, a developed and unrestricted civil society, and liberal democratic regimes. Social movements in Latin America arose in conditions of material deprivation, in stunted or constricted civil societies, and under authoritarian and often military regimes. The theory cannot therefore be applied uncritically in Latin America, because the contextual differences are too compelling. But it can be applied with caution, and with due regard for cultural and political differences; and, if it is not applied, then all the advantage of comparative analysis is lost. With scant exceptions, resource mobilization theory has not advanced beyond the confines of central capitalist society, and has perhaps been 'rejected' by Latin American and Latin Americanist researchers. In my view, this rejection is short-sighted, since this theory may have much to offer the analysis of Latin American social movements, especially the analysis of their relationship to the state. Chapter 4 begins this work. New social movement theory, in contrast, has often been applied to Latin America in a rather cavalier fashion, as if the continent has suddenly become postmodern and postmaterial. But the core concerns of the theory remain very relevant to the fast-forming and fast-changing social identities which underpin Latin America's social movements, and these concerns will be explored in the next chapter.

3 The Sociology of Social Movements

Social Movement Theory and Class Analysis

New social movement theory developed partly in response to what was considered to be an outmoded style of class analysis. The strictly class contradictions of industrial society were insufficient to describe the multiple and diverse social conflicts of postindustrial or postmodern society. Social movements do not display class characteristics, and they express social conflicts which cannot be explained in class terms. In short, the theory presumes that class analysis can no longer trace the main contours of social reality.

The intellectual history of the theory, and especially its rejection of structural Marxism, goes some way towards explaining its emphasis on social identity and identity formation. In the structuralist view, classes were composed of individuals in the same structural location, and their 'identity' was defined by external structural references. Identity was not a problem because, in the most reductionist view, classes could exist independently of social knowledge (Scott, 1991:61). But the Gramscian revolution put paid to this kind of 'objective' identity (with its implications of 'true' and 'false' consciousness) and restored social actors in modern society to a fully conscious life. Theory could then begin to catch up with an increasingly diverse social reality. Rather than an 'objectively' limited number of classes in the society, the number of social movements is limited only by the range of collective identities which people are ready to construct or willing to adopt (Boggs, 1986; Scott, 1991).

In this way social movement theory explained itself. It was the rise of social movements that provoked theoretical innovation. Touraine made an apparently radical break from class analysis by elaborating a social action theory that sees social subjects as the creators and carriers of social relations.[1] Modern society is 'self-produced' by these subjects who struggle for control over their historical context. It is this historicity which endows collective actors with more self-awareness and reflexivity (see Chapter 2). Consequently, identity is no longer an 'ascribed status' (Touraine, 1988:120), as it was in structural Marxism, but 'is defined in terms of choice', or by 'the claim to a capacity for action and for change' (Touraine, 1988:81).

Nonetheless, this break from class analysis remains ambiguous. Despite his clear preference for social movements over social classes, Touraine finally admits that 'it is impossible to give up the term classes to designate the social categories referred to by organized social movements' (Touraine, 1988:42).

The same order of ambiguity is present in much of the literature on social movements in Latin America. Social movements appear to multiply and diversify within clearly and perhaps increasingly class-divided societies. The plasticity of social movement activity contrasts dramatically with the cruel fixity of class divisions. But the ambiguity can prove useful to the analysis. If social movements in Latin America do not express class conflicts, what makes them move? If they are not themselves classes, how are they defined? More concretely, are all social protests or political demands which are not class-based an expression of social movement activity? And does the clearly class-based labour movement not qualify as a social movement (especially where authoritarian regimes have tried to constrain or remove its autonomy)? All these questions return the argument to the question of social identity. Once they have been situated in the Latin American context, the debates over 'new' identities and the process of identity-formation will be examined in more detail.

Movement and Class in Latin America

The theory suggests that the shift from classes to movements reflects the diversity of social conflicts in modern society and recognizes the legitimate existence of other identities. In Latin America 'a multiplicity of social actors establish their presence and spheres of autonomy in a fragmented social and political space' (Escobar and Alvarez, 1992:3), including 'native peoples, feminists, Christians, pacifists, ecologists, anti-racists, mothers of the disappeared, human rights activists and homosexuals' (Soto, 1989:7). Other commentaries also mention students, Catholic base communities, urban movements, and, of course, the labour movement. Moreover, any one of these categories may be highly heterogeneous. Thus, urban social movements may include transport protests, struggles for land titles, or resistance to urban planning; and may find support among popular church organizations, neighbourhood associations, or the labour movement (Machado and Ziccardi, 1983). Furthermore, differences in living situation or political orientation may produce divergent demands and partisan divisions, leading to conflicts within and between social movements (Lehmann, 1990b).

The Latin American literature often contrasts the diversity and divergence of today with the relatively limited range of social movements some 25 years ago. The 'grand actors' (Calderón et al., 1992:21) or 'large organizations' (Lehmann, 1990a) of that time included the labour, agrarian and student movements which addressed a national constituency and aimed to influence government policy. It is further suggested that these older movements corresponded to the period of import substitution industrialization, populism and the corporatist state (Lehmann, 1990a), with teachers and neighbourhood groups sometimes added to the traditional list (Soto, 1989:7). But there is some confusion whether it is the reality that has changed, or simply the definition of social movements. Escobar (Escobar and Alvarez, 1992) notes that a recent collection of essays on Mexico (Foweraker and Craig, 1990) focuses on 'more strictly defined popular actors (peasants, workers and low-income residents)', leaving aside 'ecology, feminist, gay and indigenous groups'; while Davis's review (Davis, 1989) of the collection edited by Eckstein (1989) remarks, on the contrary, that only one essay examines the labour movement, the others being dedicated to movements that 'transcend a singular class identity'.

These comments raise the central question of what or who is to be included under the general rubric of social movements. Escobar admits that the 'mosaic of forms of collective action is so diverse that one even doubts whether a single label can encompass them all' (Escobar and Alvarez, 1992:2). Yet his collection not only embraces a large variety of folk rituals, ethnic traditions and cultural phenomena in general, but also suggests that these kinds of collective action emerge 'in direct response to the post-industrial (or if one wishes post-modern) capitalist transformation' (Calderón et al., 1992:21).[2] This is supposed to demonstrate that Latin American society is finding answers to questions the analysts have not yet posed, so that there is a hidden strength in this 'fragmentation of collective action'. The new (or newly discovered) plurality of social actors is necessarily a good thing, not least because it makes of Latin America an 'extraordinary laboratory for sustained theoretical and methodological innovation' (Calderón et al., 1992:35). This seems to put the cart squarely before the horse.

Not all collective action, nor even all forms of collective protest can qualify as a social movement. Whether social conflicts in Latin America are called 'new social movements' or are demoted to mere 'popular struggles' (Touraine, 1987) they still face 'formidable problems of classification' (Assies et al., 1991). This is not just a question of the diversity or fragmentation of the movements themselves. Cardoso is correct to observe that 'movements form a unity only when we look at them from the outside looking for similarities' and that 'if we prioritize their differences they cease to form a uniform object' (Cardoso, 1987:32). Yet she still assumes that all the collective actions are movements. But if the category of social movements encompasses 'protest and conflict, lobbying and pressuring government agencies and politicians, as well as self-help development projects, of which the most frequently cited are popular education, self-built housing, consumer or product cooperatives, and community health care' (Lehmann, 1990b:150), it clearly includes too much. There is no doubt that these are forms of grass-roots and predominantly popular activity. But they compose the 'social networks', the 'recruitment networks' or the 'micromobilization contexts' (see Chapter 2) which provide the social and cognitive preconditions for movement emergence. They are not social movements themselves. These strictures may apply equally to traditional activities of a cultural kind and to new organizations like Catholic base communities, that, depending on context and circumstances, may or may not act as 'pre-movements'.[3]

Therefore social movements cannot be coterminous with social protest or, still less, with social life in general. On the contrary, their social scope is usually rather limited. Yet 'in social scientific writings, movements tend to become, as if by magic, "the people", the "town" or the "locale", as though there were not enormous differences – and enormously complex relations – between participants and nonparticipants' (Burdick, 1992:183). One exception is Mainwaring's study of the *Movimento dos Amigos do Bairro* in Nova Iguaçú, a powerful movement which organized some 160 neighbourhood associations (Mainwaring, 1989). Total membership of the movement was never more than about 8,000 people, with possibly as many as 40,000 participating at one time or another. This meant that an absolute maximum of 3 per cent of the population had ever participated in the movement, and most had never even heard of it. As Tarrow suggests of his 'moments of madness', 'those involved in them only suppose themselves to be at the center of a world turned upside down; in actual fact, most other people are going about their business as usual' (Tarrow, 1987:7). On the other hand, it is equally important to recognize the specificity of social movements where they exist, and to reject the assumption that they are all simply 'component parts' of one massive movement (Eyerman and Jamison, 1991:91).[4]

Once social movements are recognized as both different from social activity in general and different one from the other, it is possible to assess the competing claims of social movement theory and class analysis. Urban social movements, for example, are said to draw support from a highly differentiated class structure which includes the classical working class, street vendors, casual labour, small scale (familial) enterprise, informal petty bourgeoisie and an informal service sector (Pansters, 1986). Since urban populations all suffer equally from low incomes and inadequate services and utilities, the identity or 'consciousness' of the movements is rooted not in class but in their common experiences within the defined social space which is the *barrio* or neighbourhood. But other studies suggest that these movements are still divided along class lines, that very few movements involve both middle and popular classes, that middle class and popular demands diverge radically, and that urban movements are usually a mixture of sectors of the working class and shanty-town dwellers of different kinds (Boschi, 1987b). In other words, social heterogeneity has its limits. In exceptional cases like the Federation of Neighbourhood Associations of the State of Rio de Janeiro (FAMERJ), the most effective state-wide movement in Brazil, the class lines were crossed, but even FAMERJ did not represent *favela* or shanty-town organizations. Extrapolating from the urban context, it seems safe to suggest that some class content subsists in most social mobilization, and that social movement identity will be a complex composition of class, spatial, religious, national or other elements. Hence, 'class struggles can combine with cross-class aspects of gender, ethnic, generational and other struggles in important and potentially powerful ways' (Chinchilla, 1992:45), just as social movements can be driven in some degree by class conflicts. To what degree is an empirical question.

The Newness of New Social Movements

One of the main contentions of the new social movements thesis is that these movements are new because they do not have the clear class base of older labour or agrarian movements, and because they do not have a special interest appeal to any one group. In the Latin American context it is alleged that the predominance of labour and peasant movements before and during the 1960s was progressively undermined by the rise of urban social movements during the 1970s (Mainwaring, 1987), while in Europe the new movements respond to the diffuse concerns of a variegated middle class (Offe, 1985). This middle class is seen as more susceptible to the perverse effects of modernization or, as in Inglehart's notion of 'cognitive mobilization' (Inglehart, 1977), better able to interpret them.

In this thesis the labour movement, in particular, is associated with the neocorporatist framework of collaboration between state agencies and trade unions. New social movements, on the other hand, refuse this kind of collaboration, and eschew the conventional politics of interest intermediation, political parties and elections (Dalton and Keuchler, 1990). In short, 'whereas prior social movements fought to secure political and economic rights from the state and other institutional actors, new social movements target their activities away from the state' (D'Anieri and Kier, 1990:446). To play with 'politics' is to risk cooptation by corporate-industrial organizations, so the new movements focus their energies on mobilizing resources and publicizing the issues. 'Like sharks, they have to keep moving to stay alive' (Dalton and Keuchler, 1990:16). They use the political pressure of public opinion and protest activities, orchestrating their protests to gain maximum media coverage.

Thus, whereas the labour movement developed a formal organization, sought political integration and political rights, and operated within the political system, new social movements are supposed to employ direct action, promote changes in dominant values, and move mainly within civil society (Scott, 1991). They do not challenge the state directly, but by their expressive politics they demonstrate the limited processing capacity of 'normal politics' (Offe, 1990). They reject political negotiation in favour of collective claims on identity and personal liberation (Melucci, 1989). Hence, for the new feminist movement it is not equal pay and political rights which define the agenda so much as female autonomy and professional development (D'Anieri and Kier, 1990). In general, Cohen concludes, it is the 'autonomous, voluntary, and indigenous associations within civil society using and expanding public discourse and public spaces for discourse [that] are the *differentia specifica* of contemporary social movements' (Cohen and Arato, 1992:494).

In the European context, the newness of these social movements is derived from the new forms of subordination typical of late capitalism: the commodification of social life, or the expansion of capitalist relations into culture, leisure and sexuality; the bureaucratization of society; and the massification or homogenization of social life by the invasive power of the mass media (Mouffe, 1988). These restatements of Habermas' original insights into the different attacks on the 'organic foundations of the lifeworld' (Slater, 1991) are used to explain the multiplication of 'sites of struggle' inside modern society and outside of the production process. In Latin America, very differently, the newness of the movements is seen to derive from the crisis of the developmentalist and populist state in Mexico and South America (or the oligarchic state in Central America) in the 1960s (Escobar and Alvarez, 1992:4). Their emergence is then explained by the advent of repressive military regimes (which suppressed alternative forms of political organization like trade unions and political parties), the crisis of the traditional left (for similar reasons), the rejection of populist politics, and the 'demonstration effect' of new movements in the United States and Europe (Assies et al., 1991). Their newness is therefore defined negatively by their relative independence of both the old pattern of populist politics and the political programmes of revolutionary vanguards.

But if the origin is different, the results in Latin America are said to look somewhat similar. In the 1960s, it is suggested, social movements were strongly oriented towards the state, but today the state is no longer an 'object of attraction' (Escobar and Alvarez, 1992). Instead the movements are looking for 'new ways of doing politics' and 'new places for doing politics' (Assies et al., 1991:3), and this implies a 'search for cultural identities and spaces for social expression' (Escobar and Alvarez, 1992:5). In this perspective it is easy to reproduce the dichotomous schemes of European theory. 'New social movements are inclined towards affective concerns, expressive relations, group orientation, and horizontal organization. Old social movements are inclined towards material concerns, instrumental relations, orientation towards the state, and vertical organization' (Mainwaring and Viola, 1984:20). But even a careful selection of minority movements like the ecology and pacifist movements (Scherer-Warren and Krische, 1987), or 'premovements' like Catholic base communities provide no convincing evidence for these assertions, while urban social movements or urban or rural union movements are both concerned with material issues and closely involved with state apparatuses and agencies. The very different relations between state and civil society in Latin America (see Chapter 2) do make a difference: if social movements in Latin America are new in presenting a challenge to the political culture of paternalism and clientelism (Assies et al., 1991), the challenge cannot be mounted at a great distance from the state (see Chapter 4).

Yet the theorists appear confident that the European movements are 'new', both because they embody new values and because they aspire to bring about change by changing values (Melucci, 1989). A general shift from material to post material values (Inglehart, 1977) means less emphasis on economic concerns and more preoccupation with cultural issues. Instead of the instrumental pursuit of specific and economic-corporate demands (Gramsci, 1973) the new movements aim to achieve collective results or 'goods' that cannot be restricted to movement members (so violating the restraints of Olson's implacable calculus) (Dalton and Keuchler, 1990). This is understood as a

global response to the unwelcome trends of economic stag-
nation, ecological destruction, militarism and bureaucratic politics (Boggs, 1986). It is therefore the politicization of new
issues that makes the movements 'progressive' (Offe, 1990),[5]
and changes the content of 'left' and 'right' politics. Since the
new issues do not crystallize into a positive utopia of a 'new
society', many believe that the traditional left/right divisions no
longer describe the political spectrum. In place of utopia, the
movements focus on themselves (D'Anieri and Kier, 1990:446),
and especially their autonomy from political intervention and
bureaucratic control (Offe, 1985). This makes their activities
'symbolic' (Melucci, 1989) or 'expressive' (Dalton and Keuchler,
1990) in nature, although there is recurrent reference in the
literature to the tension between the quest for change and the
pragmatic constraints of 'doing politics'.

These new values imply a totally different style of political
organization. Whereas labour unions and (some) civil rights
groups are seen to have a centralized, hierarchical and often
clientelist structure, the organization of the new movements is
variously described as decentralized, nonhierarchical, anti-oligar-
chical, open, spontaneous, fluid and participatory. It is suggested that very different movements, like the women's and
anti-war movements in the United States or the anti-nuclear
and student movements in Europe, all have this loose style of
organization in common (Scott, 1991). This informal style may
be understood as a result of the similarly 'loose' social networks
which underpin the movements, of an ideological commitment
to direct democracy and cooperative decision-making (especially
in the environmental, women's and peace movements), or of the
emphasis on 'lifestyle' issues, and on personal learning and
liberation. Taken together, these organizational and ideological
characteristics create an implicit challenge to the 'microphysics
of power' (Foucault, 1977; Foweraker, 1989a). In this perspective resource mobilization theory's preoccupation with the
political efficacy of the movements is not the only question.
What movements are is as important as what they do. The
movement is the message.

Continuities from 'Old' to 'New' Social Movements

Some theorists deny the newness of new social movements. The
assertion of newness is founded on wrong assumptions about the
nature of the 'old' movements (D'Anieri and Kier, 1990).[6] If the
characteristics of the 'new' movements are not in fact new, then
they cannot be explained by deep changes in the social system,

whether from liberal to late capitalism (Habermas, 1973), from industrial to post industrial society (Touraine, 1988), or from production to reproduction (Castells, 1983). There is a tendency to reify the original impulse to mobilize rather than the movements' formation and development. The emphasis on loose organization, participation and non-negotiable demands privileges the radical elements within the movements at the moment of their emergence (Scott, 1991). In fact, all movements begin informally and develop some degree of formal organization (although this remains highly variable between and within movements). All movements press for participation and employ expressive and confrontational tactics at some point in their trajectory (Tarrow, 1988b) (and some degree of violence characterizes mass mobilization from pre-industrial times to the present) (Mueller, 1992). And both 'old' and 'new' movements come to focus, sooner or later, on citizenship concerns. Hence, 'new social movements' is not a tenable sociological category, and their so-called 'unique' features are typical of social movements as such. In fact, these 'new' social movements simply continue the job of the 'old' movements. 'They open up the political sphere, they articulate popular demands and they politicize issues previously confined to the private realm' (Scott, 1991:155).

The implicit or explicit comparison for the new social movements is always the labour movement. But this movement was equally marked by the tension between radical demands and the practical constraints of pragmatic politics, and it is the political thrust of the movements which proves the continuities. The labour movement made the employment contract political just as the women's movement makes gender relations political (Scott, 1991). In the cases of the student, women's, environmental and peace movements 'we see a deep interpenetration of old and new and a progressive politicization that led several of the movements into the area of the party system' (Klandermans et al., 1988); and Charles Tilly and others have discovered a cooccurrence between social movement activity and increases in conventional political participation which again suggests that the stark division between old and new may be overdrawn (Tarrow, 1988b). In particular, the supposedly distinctive cultural concerns of the new social movements have clear political implications, while the labour movement can still mount political protests which look just as new as those of any other contemporary movement (Pizzorno, 1978). Moreover, social movements frequently start from insurgencies within existing organizations (Zald and Berger, 1987), and nowhere more so than within organized and corporatized trade unions. Such 'syndical movements' (Touraine, 1987) have been crucial to the recent political history of Spain, Brazil and Mexico.

The comparison with the labour movement carries the implication (noted in the first section of this chapter) that the new movements, unlike the old, are not class-based. But the European theorists also suggest that the new movements are based in the educated middle class (or in the most privileged sectors of less privileged groups), and especially in the 'third generation' which has been excluded from political decision-making (Scott, 1991). Therefore the new movements are indeed class organizations which, just like old class organizations, appeal to general principles beyond specific class interests. Moreover, if they are drawn from the middle class, so are many of the intellectuals and activists of the old movements (Tarrow, 1988b). In fact, the class basis of many movements from the ecology movement in Italy (Diani and Lodi, 1988) to urban social movements in Latin America (Castells, 1977) may be mixed and variegated, and their strategic trajectory will then be shaped to secure a variety of class alliances. The complexities of the class-movement relationship are also seen as a constant of social movement activity, especially amongst those who favour cyclical theories of social mobilization (Brand, 1990).

Social Movements and the Construction of Identity

European theorists have stressed the reflexivity of new social movements, meaning their inclination and capacity to interrogate their own identity. This is the central question for Melucci, not only as a precondition of effective action but as a goal in its own right (Gamson, 1992). Social mobilization is no longer achieved by the 'historical personalities' of yesteryear, such as the labour movement, because such coherent collective actors no longer exist (Melucci, 1989). Hence political struggle inevitably involves 'the search for different identities' (Jelin, 1990), or articulates different attempts to reassert control over individual and collective identity (D'Anieri and Kier, 1990).

The notion of searching for identity is simply a metaphor for collective action as a process of identity construction. A social movement cannot be treated as a 'unitary empirical datum' (Melucci, 1988) or 'single actor' (Tilly, 1985) that represents a coherent group of some kind and needs no further inquiry. On the contrary, this relatively unified actor is 'a problem to be explained' by the 'elements of structure and motivation that can combine in a variable manner' (Melucci, 1988:331). In other words collective actors 'are created in the course of social movement activity' (Taylor and Whittier, 1992) and 'the interaction among actors constitutes the identity and unity of the movement' (Tilly, 1985:736). But this cannot be a fixed result because the 'closure', in the Weberian sense, which defines who is in and who is out will vary over time. Social movement success may transform a collective identity into public goods available to everyone, and so no longer exclusive to the movement (Snow and Benford, 1992). Self-evidently, the broader and more variegated an identity, the less restricted the field of potential participants, and vice versa.

The preoccupation with identity is said to be the result of 'an increasingly fragmented and pluralistic social reality' (Taylor and Whittier, 1992:110) which social movements themselves contribute to create (see Chapter 2). But the fragmentation is also internal to the movements. 'The group image is a mystification. In real social movements, involvement ebbs and flows, coalitions form and dissolve, fictitious organizations loom up and fade away, (and) would-be leaders compete for recognition as the representatives of unorganized constituencies' (Tilly, 1984:312). Every movement has to contend with a 'plurality of orientations' (Melucci, 1988:331) or 'subject positions' (Laclau and Mouffe, 1985) which may feed on or facilitate internal tensions and divisions of a political or personal nature; and even if such positions are expressed ideologically, they may be rooted in an implacably material reality. In urban Brazil, for example, levels of consumption are so unequal, and spatial segregation and access to public services so distorted, that urban social movements cannot easily construct alliances beyond their own communities. Their demands are so immediate and their goals so diverse that it is 'impossible to construct a general model of grassroots movements in contemporary Brazil' (Mainwaring, 1989:169). 'To the outside (social movements) may present varying degrees of unity, but internally they are always heterogeneous, with very diverse meanings, forms of action and organizations' (Jelin, 1990:5).

Collective actors cannot simply be understood, therefore, as recognizing and representing common and defined interests. 'Political dissent does not represent identities and interests, it produces them' (Assies et al., 1991:118, paraphrasing the argument of Laclau and Mouffe, 1985). Hence the appeal to identity 'is an appeal to a non-social definition of the social actor' (Touraine, 1988:75), so that social movements only occur if actors can 'acknowledge and assert themselves as producers rather than consumers of social situations' (Touraine, 1988:11). It is not necessary to accept Touraine's ambitious definition of social movements (as aspiring to the social management of political culture and the activities it produces) to recognize the moment of the assertion of identity. By achieving such identities social movements produce an age of 'contested subordination' (Laclau and Mouffe, 1985), and, according to Touraine, create the preconditions for representative democracy. Democracy is weak in Latin America because social actors are so often 'not only controlled but created by the state' (Touraine, 1987), whereas democracy requires not just representative institutions but 'actors who are defined, organized and capable of action before they have any channel of political representation' (Touraine, 1988:151) (see Chapter 5).

But it is not always clear whether it is the social actors or the theorists who are more preoccupied with the question of identity. The theorists' insistence on the multiplication of identities may simply gloss the kind of communal, neighbourly or local relations that have been the stuff of social life for centuries. In short, 'one may detect in these conceptions a certain dose of normativism and even utopianism' (Escobar and Alvarez, 1992:81). Hence it is important to remember that every identity is 'socially constructed through a collective context' (Mueller, 1992) which always begins 'at the molecular level of interpersonal relations' (Weffort, 1989) and of primary social networks.[7] It is often a sense of neighbourhood that sustains urban social movements in Latin America, and this is created through intense networking and complex relations of exchange and reciprocity. This communalism is the core of neighbourhood identity and a precondition of presenting common demands (Pansters, 1986). For the women who are the majority presence in the urban movements 'intra-community social networks are far more important politically than parties or trade unions', and the key components of community organization (house meetings, publicity, community research and political action) 'all depend on verbal communication and personal contact' (Corcoran-Nantes, 1990). These networks catalyse social mobilization and facilitate cooperation between different movements within the same neighbourhood.

Social networks compose a 'submerged reality' which is the latent or less readily observed side of social mobilization (Melucci, 1988:248). This reality has been variously described in terms of subcultures, alternative milieu, issue-specific publics, movement networks and social movement sectors (Dalton and Keuchler, 1990). But what does it contain? Tarrow conceives of this sector as action oriented so that its shape and composition will vary over time 'as groups mobilize and demobilize, issues move on and off the political agenda, and elites respond with different combinations of facilitation, repression, indifference and reform' (Tarrow, 1988a:432). An exclusive focus on organizations might 'conventionalize' the informal and spontaneous aspects of social mobilization, but organizations like labour unions and religious groups can certainly move in and out of the sector. Moreover, 'there are often one or two movements that color the preoccupations and methods used by other movements during the era' (Tarrow, 1988a:432). One such movement to emerge in contemporary Mexico was the teachers' movement, which initiated tactics and strategies that were later adopted by other movements, and that occasionally acted as a vanguard for broader-based social protests (Foweraker, 1993).

More typical of the 'social movement sector' in Latin America were the Catholic base communities in Brazil that, during the harshest period of military rule, 'were virtually the only popular organizations which developed critical political perspectives' (Mainwaring and Viola, 1984:27). More accurately, they came to provide some social and political succour as other organizations were suppressed, and, by some estimates, there were as many as 80,000 of them across the country by the early 1980s. Crucially, they were the source of many neighbourhood associations, and communities and associations combined in offering support to the 'new unionism' in São Paulo just as communities and the popular church were closely linked to rural unionism in the Amazon region. In Chile, on the other hand, since the Catholic Church played an important but less decentralized and prophetic role (Lehmann, 1990b), the bulk of the sector was composed of different kinds of survival or self-help organizations which proliferated throughout greater Santiago. By 1987 there were some 1,400 such groups, including communal kitchens, workshops and consumer cooperatives, with as many as 50,000 active members. Such organizations are ephemeral but effective in nurturing submerged social networks.

More specific than the social movement sector overall is the local, regional or cross-cultural 'activists' network' (Kriesi, 1988:46) which is fully committed to the 'social movement industry' (McCarthy and Zald, 1973). Such networks are composed of individuals who dedicate themselves full-time to organizing social movement activity, and who may participate in several movements over the course of their career. Many Latin American activists had managed to build national and international connections. Among them were activists who had been exiled abroad, especially in the 'North', leaders of the popular church who joined the debate and practice of liberation theology, and intellectuals and academics within various research centres in Chile, Brazil, Argentina and Peru, who were engaged in the kind of 'action research' most favoured and financed by international NGOs. These different sorts of activists could all provide political leadership for social movements and create a sense of political significance that went far beyond the confines of the immediate community.

These different orders of social network also enter the cultural construction of social movements. It has become axiomatic that the movements cannot be defined by social and political categories alone, but must also be seen as 'cultural' (Escobar and Alvarez, 1992:7). In the first place, this simply suggests that social movement 'actors produce meanings, communicate, negotiate, and make decisions', and that much of this activity will go unnoticed if 'political reductionism' is allowed to dismiss it as 'uninteresting, unmeasurable, expressive, folkloristic, and so on' (Melucci, 1988:336–7). In other words, 'cultural politics' involves 'struggles over meaning at the level of daily life' (Escobar and Alvarez, 1992:71), and these struggles begin within the social networks. But they are also informed by the 'collective action frames' or loosely organized systems of ideas which link individuals to social movements and to each other (Snow and Benford, 1992:143), so shaping the movements and even entire 'protest cycles'. 'Collective action is thus the stage on which new meanings are produced, as well as a text full of old meanings' (Tarrow, 1989). Since the exercise of 'hegemony' (Gramsci, 1973) will restrict the meanings necessary to motivate social mobilization, a cultural interpretation can therefore claim that 'the symbolic reach of movements ... often exceeds their social reach or measurable impact' (Escobar and Alvarez, 1992:328).[8]

The cultural impact of social movements also occurs at the level of the individual and, again, it is social networks that link individual life experience with the organization and strategy of the movement (Foweraker, 1989a; 1993). The original impulse may be the reassertion 'of one's own dignity, *vis-à-vis* the everyday experience of misery, oppression and cultural devastation' (Assies et al., 1991), but the key step is to connect 'personal troubles' to 'public issues' (Mills, 1959) by seeking a social solution to individual anguish (as Marx suggested in the 1844 Manuscripts). In doing so the individual changes personal identity by joining the movement and 'taking on' its collective identity that then functions both as 'a public pronouncement of status' and 'an individual announcement of affiliation, of connection to others' (Friedman and McAdam, 1992:157). Inevitably this collective identity will be shaped in part (but only in part) by the individuals who make up the movement, but the point here is that individual participation is a 'potentially transformative experience' (Friedman and McAdam, 1992) which can create loyalty to the movement and commitment to the cause. The transformation does not happen naturally but through mobilization, struggle and face-to-face encounters. In addition, many movements in Latin America use propaganda, leaflets, radio, comics and street theatre to promote popular education.

Above all the transformation is catalysed by the myriad leadership roles created by 'social movement sector' organizations like
the popular church and neighbourhood associations.

The transformative potential of social movements recalls the
philosophy of anarchism, with its emphasis on self-management,
basist democracy, and respect for individual and community identities; and its critique of the bureaucratic centralism,
authoritarianism and dogma of traditional political organizations
(Scherer-Warren and Krische, 1987:36). The influence of anarchism on contemporary social movements has long been recognized
in Europe, and especially in Spain (Foweraker, 1989), but the
resemblance between modern and anarchist movements has only
recently been noted in Latin America (Fals Borda, 1986; Fuentes
and Frank, 1989). Although anarchism is often criticized for its
utopianism in a world of increasing state power, it may be a
better starting point than traditional Marxism for understanding
the links between individual and collective identity, and between
the conquest of individual and collective autonomy.

Social Movements in Civil Society

The emphasis on identity can imply that social movements are
uniquely concerned to form themselves as collective subjects within
civil society. By doing so they may achieve social and cultural
change at the grassroots of this society without any interaction with
the state (Karnen, 1987). They press their demands through 'non-
institutional channels' (Jelin, 1990), and remain incapable of instig-
ating institutional change. They insist on their political autonomy
even if it leads to isolation, impotence and the retreat to 'reactionary utopias' (Castells, 1983:328; Hannigan, 1985), but this cannot
be the end of the story. Social movements, especially in Latin
America, cannot escape the state entirely. Whether it is a human
rights movement confronting state terror in Argentina or an urban
movement challenging state paternalism in Brazil, every movement
is marked by its political environment (see Chapter 4). In short,
'social movements are situated ... in the intermediate space between
individualized, familiar, habitual, micro-climatic daily life, and
socio-political processes writ large, of the State and the institutions,
solemn and superior' (Jelin, 1987).

In this connection it must be clear that identity is formed in
some degree through political struggle, and so shaped by relations of political power. Such power is not confined to the
realm of the state but is present in, and reproduced through,
the social relations of civil society. Hence this society is not a
simple 'space of freedom' quite separate from the state (see

Chapter 2), and the notion of 'nonpolitical' social movements is difficult to defend (Telles, 1987). Poor residents of the urban periphery in Latin America seek to assure their own survival by building their own dwellings in the classic pattern of self-help housing. But, in conditions of speculation and corruption, illegal occupation is often the only way to secure a plot of land, and such 'invasions' are the founding moment of many urban movements. The movements come to focus on the struggle for land titles, and are inevitably drawn into the legal and institutional sphere of the state. Even if successful, they will continue to confront the power relations implicit in their conditions of life, pitting their common enterprise against the impersonal logic of 'the system'. Identity will then be formed cumulatively through the experience and memory of struggles past and present. This identity is unlikely to remain more pure or unsullied than the political world around it.

Just as social movements are sometimes seen to be confined to civil society, so their mobilization is alleged to be expressive rather than instrumental. This is supposed to be true of women's groups, urban movements, and their combinations, such as the Cost of Living Movement in the São Paulo of the 1970s. But the repressive conditions of military-authoritarian Latin America have tended to muddy the dividing line between expressive and instrumental action. The restrictions on new actors and new forms of organization, and the direct repression of social movements, tended to imbue all mobilization with an expressive, and even emotional and heroic content. This does not mean that all social mobilization is the same. Some will be more expressive and affirming of identity or community (such as protests on behalf of the 'disappeared'); some will be more instrumental and designed to win material benefits (such as land seizures and strikes); and some will be directly political and designed to bring down the regime (such as the *diretas já* campaign in Brazil) (Garretón, 1989b). But it does mean that all such mobilization is some sort of mixture of the expressive and the instrumental, which, in Latin America at least, always combine together (Cardoso, 1983:235).

This indicates that it is never easy to separate the practices that sustain identity and strategy. Any process of mobilization means that 'converts must be sought, resources acquired and the commitment of members maintained'. But it is the strategic approach to political authorities and strategic success that will best ensure 'an ongoing sense of legitimacy and efficacy among movement cadres and members' (McAdam et al., 1988:722). In other words, goals, tactics and strategic choices not only impact on the political environment but also shape the way issues are seen within the movement, and so achieve lesser or greater degrees of loyalty and cohesion. Conversely, it is only with the achievement of an organized identity that protest or strategic action becomes possible. This sort of mobilization 'depends upon a previously constituted social organization ... (and) requires the prior formation of close social ties ... (and) the formation of organizations' (Birnbaum, 1988:24); and 'the stronger the group's feeling of identity ... the more organized the group is' (Birnbaum, 1988:29, referring to Tilly's research). Although not everyone is convinced by the latter argument,[9] it remains impossible to disentangle the intrinsic (identity) and extrinsic (strategy) practices of social movements, even if they may be addressed separately for heuristic purposes (Foweraker, 1993:2–15).

Just as the theorists may have overestimated the spontaneity of social movements (and mistaken their absence of interaction with the state), so they have underestimated the importance of external leaders to movement emergence and success. Cardoso is categorical that the social movements of Latin America would not exist in their present form were it not for the crucial role played by lawyers, teachers, doctors, architects and the pastoral agents of the popular church in providing political guidance and technical support and assistance (Cardoso, 1983:231). The popular or 'informal' church, whether within Catholic base communities or not, has been especially effective in motivating grassroots mobilization and promoting human rights groups in Chile and Brazil.[10] Church leaders, alongside teachers and social workers, have an almost natural place 'inside' the local community. They share the common experience of misery and oppression; they understand local realities; they promote and participate in 'basist' or directly democratic decision-making. Union and (left-wing) party leaders, on the other hand, are seen as exercising influence from the 'outside', and are tainted by a general suspicion of political parties and bureaucratic agencies. The presence of different external agents can lead to competition, or even conflict between them. This exacerbates the difficulties of achieving any form of legitimate leadership for local movements which favour a participatory style and egalitarian values.

One of the most important components of identity is rarely mentioned in the literature, and that is the presence of distinct political generations. This is critical to the role of external leaderships. In Mexico the veterans of the student movement of 1968 became the leaders of community struggles and regional movements in subsequent years, so 'seeding' a whole generation of social mobilization across the country, especially in urban social movements and the teachers' movement (Perez Arce, 1990; Foweraker, 1993). Similarly in Brazil it was the survivors of the failed struggles of the 1960s (from the Catholic left, the revolutionary left and the more militant unions) who carried the lessons of those struggles into the Catholic base communities and urban neighbourhoods of the 1970s (Telles, 1987). In Chile too the grassroots leaders of the 1960s remained active in resisting the dictatorship, and the areas of fiercest urban struggle corresponded to the previously most militant left-wing neighbourhoods. The capacity of these communities 'to mobilize mass political resistance, despite ten years of severe military repression, lay in the political heritage of decades of work in the popular culture in the formation of a skilled generation of grass-roots militants' (Schneider, 1992:263). So effective was this work that militants who were killed or imprisoned could always be replaced by youths who were heirs to the same tradition. In this way such generations could instil resilience in the movements, while also creating the kind of long-term vision that might correct the immediatism of many movement objectives.

The Women's Movements of Latin America

These general questions of identity formation and the role of social movements in (re)constructing civil society will now be pursued in relation to the women's movements of the continent. There are strong a priori grounds for focusing on women, for there is little doubt that the social mobilization of women in contemporary Latin America is new in its degree, its forms and its ideological expression. Women's mobilization began to increase rapidly from the mid-1970s, and within 10 years it had reached levels that were unprecedented in Latin American history. In Argentina, Brazil, Chile, Peru and Mexico women succeeded in vindicating a new space for themselves in local and national political life. In Guatemala, Salvador and Nicaragua they swelled the cadres of revolutionary organizations. Although there was some mobilization of rural women in countries like Peru and Nicaragua, which had undergone agrarian reforms, most women were active in the urban setting, and participated in a range of grassroots organizations that were mainly geared to 'building a community' (Caldeira, 1990:48). The awareness of common needs and the construction of consensus were mainly achieved within the community as the 'basic organizing unit' (Corcoran-Nantes, 1990:225) of urban movements that were always 'territorially based' (Schuurman, 1989). Hence, 'whether or not a movement appears depends mainly on ... the strength of feeling in the community' (Corcoran-Nantes, 1990:225). Communal feelings tended to focus on the provision of public services and public utilities, and on tax, consumption and cost-of-living issues in general. In short, women's mobilization did not respond primarily to any particular church doctrine, party programme or ideology and, in most cases, women were firm in suggesting that their protests had no political goals or ambitions. Thus, the ideological content of women's mobilization had also changed.

This unprecedented degree of mobilization made women the majority presence in most urban social movements. Movements in São Paulo, Brazil, 'are in the main constituted and led by women' (Caldeira, 1990), who are said to make up some 80 per cent of all participants (Corcoran-Nantes, 1990). In Rio de Janeiro, women headed a quarter of all middle-class associations by the early 1980s (Boschi, 1987). In Mexico, women compose a clear majority within most urban movements, as well as forming their vanguard in some cases (Moctezuma, 1984; Massolo and Ronner, 1983). In Lima, Peru, women had mobilized massively in support of teachers and public sector employees in the early 1980s, and by 1986 there were some 100,000 women participating in the municipal milk programme, with many more staffing the 600 or so communal kitchens (Jaquette, 1989). In virtually all cases 'the political expression of the movement was bound up with the group's identification with its place of residence' (Boschi, 1987), and the mobilizing issues were always those of survival and service provision. Hence women were active in demanding schools, nurseries, clinics, health care, land titles, transport, and basic services for shanty towns; and in protesting price increases, tax hikes, and local government or police interference in their communities. In Chile, women were especially hard hit by the combination of economic contraction and political repression (Kirkwood, 1983),[11] and they responded by setting up soup kitchens, consumer cooperatives and workshops, so that by 1985 there were some 1,100 of these 'popular economic organizations' in Santiago (Jaquette, 1989). In the changing context of economic crisis, growing debt and IMF austerity programmes, women sought alternative ways of accomplishing their traditional tasks of satisfying basic needs and generating family income. Their participation in the 'informal' economy was now 'formalized' through community-based services like those in Chile and Peru, and through neighbourhood associations and urban movements (Safa, 1990).

It is evident that women were mobilizing around practical gender interests, defined as those interests that 'arise (inductively) from the concrete conditions of women's position within the gender division of labour' (Molyneaux, 1985). These interests do not entail a strategic goal but focus on basic needs and immediate concerns such as the care of children. It is mainly poor women of the urban periphery who are mobilized by these concerns (Molyneaux, 1985), and the women's movement, or feminism as such, had small success in reaching the poor districts of Latin American cities (Jaquette, 1989). But even if women of the urban periphery are not part of the feminist movement, or not aware of its message, they have come to reject violence against women and to insist 'on the right of women to leave the household in order to participate in the neighbourhood association and base community' (Mainwaring and Viola, 1984:39). In other words, despite the 'practicality' of their concerns, their mobilization must lead to negotiated changes in the domestic sphere, and therefore in the quality of their everyday lives.

Women are struggling to defend their community, protect their children and improve their living conditions. But by 'struggling for their own good' they also begin to escape the isolation and frequent loneliness of the home, and so start to 'lose their fear' (Caldeira, 1990:72). Their participation in the more 'formal' survival activities is a means to education, self-development, friendship and a new 'sociability'; and in this way the urban movements empower women by catalysing 'new forms of social relations and social organizations' (Jelin, 1990:3).[12] One example is the effort women put into researching their own conditions in order to negotiate more effectively with municipal and other authorities. This research was a 'female political strategy' that developed both the movements and the women themselves (Corcoran-Nantes, 1990:261). Hence, for women, 'the really novel aspect of recent social movements is that as a form of engaging in politics they affect daily life and modify it' (Caldeira, 1990:72). Their private life begins to impinge on the public world, and their social existence takes on political overtones. Rather than follow the dictates of union bosses, party leaders or church officials, women had begun to seek more autonomous forms of organization where their own voice could be heard. Beyond any local successes in the struggle against impoverishment and indigence, their mobilization caused a sea-change in their lives, from passivity to combativeness (Jelin, 1990). Ignoring the risk of repression, women increasingly came to assemble, march, demonstrate, and so to maintain a collective and public presence at all moments of political confrontation.

Redefining the Private/Public Division

If struggles within the urban environment are seen uniquely in terms of class and capital, then women tend to be excluded from the analysis. The woman who is wife, mother and housewife is subordinated and isolated; the woman who cooks, washes and cleans is relegated to the private or personal sphere. Despite urban sociology's general notions of 'social reproduction' women remain absent from the public sphere and are made invisible (Massolo and Ronner, 1983). But this deep division between the private and public spheres is breaking down. Economic crisis, austerity programmes and cuts in state services have brought more women into the labour force or into multiform self-help activities. The invasion of family life by authoritarian regimes has broken the spell of domestic security (Safa, 1990). In Habermasian terms (see Chapter 2) the private and civil domain of the family has been rapidly colonized by increasing state and market intervention. It is alleged that these processes precipitate the atomization and individualization of civil society, and so prevent collective action (Oszlak, 1987). But it was precisely the private or 'traditional' roles of the woman that were now projected into public and community organization. Housewives mobilized to provide affordable food and pick up where state services left off; mothers mobilized on behalf of family members who had 'disappeared' (Valenzuela, 1990), their private grief impelling public protest (Feijoó, 1989). Domesticity was redefined to include participation and struggle rather than obedience and passivity. And all this had profound implications for the women themselves, 'releasing them from lives that are "naturally determined" to enter the "socially determined" world, where they can be the subjects, not merely the objects, of political action' (Jaquette, 1989:189).

But there are costs. Women at the heart of urban social movements had been seen in the 'doubly difficult situation of exploited workers and deprived residents' (Ramírez Saiz, 1987). With their commitment to political struggle they are now seen to have not just a double but a triple burden of home, work and community organization (Moser, 1987). Women continue to pay the personal price for inadequate services, spending hours of their lives waiting for the water truck or the garbage truck; or finding ways to build community services where state support is quite lacking. At the same time they are workers for poor wages, and simultaneously engaged in different forms of domestic production. Finally they have to negotiate the complex terrain of clientelistic and patrimonial relations of their newly political world in order to get their demands heard and possibly met, and this process is often attended by frustration, indignities and even humiliation. The accumulation of physical and psychological pressures can be overwhelming (Massolo, 1989).

Possibly for this reason, among others, women tend to adopt a different style of organization, promoting collective leadership and shared decision-making, in contrast to the vertical lines of command that characterize male-dominated political parties and trade unions (Lehmann, 1990b). 'Struggling for one's own good' takes place in the community, where everyone is equal and where all demands are concrete. This is a female space of 'women's talk', and the social mobilization that follows is not seen as political. On the contrary, politics is a remote and foreign world of abstract debate and struggles for personal power (Caldeira, 1990). Above all it is a male domain of parties and unions and 'men's politics' (Safa, 1990) which is alien to women's needs. Moreover, this distinction facilitates women's mobilization and makes it more genuinely social. Even though social movement theory tends to see women 'through the very political institutional perspective from which they tend to distance themselves ... for them the new form of activism found in social movements is considered not to be politics but a new way of experiencing the condition of womanhood' (Caldeira, 1990:72).

But it is politics, if a different kind of politics. The Mothers of the Plaza de Mayo in Argentina emerged in direct response to state terrorism and kidnapping. A relatively small number of mainly middle-class women mobilized around the non-negotiable demand for human rights, and especially the right to life. The protest was not partisan (the Mothers refused to join any political party) or doctrinaire (they espoused no political or ideological programme). It was driven by a purely ethical imperative as motherhood became the basis of political militancy. It cannot be denied that the rejection of all violence and the affirmation of life was 'expressive', especially insofar as it destroyed the myth of female submissiveness. But no rational actor model can easily explain mobilization that involved so much sacrifice (the symbolism of motherhood did not make the Mothers safe from violence and repression). Perhaps for this reason the (male) military government never suspected that the protest could be effective. In its view these were *locas*, or 'mad women', who did not understand the realities of political power.

It is a long way from the historic central square of Buenos Aires to the highlands of Bolivia, where the mobilization of peasant women had increased enormously during the Banzer dictatorship of 1971–8. Following massive female participation in the road blockades of 1979, the First Congress of Peasant Women in January 1980 founded the Bartolina Sisa Union Federation of Peasant Women. The women were responding in part to economic pressures, and in part to the experience of dictatorship and the necessity of defending democracy. But this was not the whole story. Bartolina Sisa had been the *compañera* of Tupac Katari during the anticolonial struggles of the eighteenth century, and the Katarista movement had worked to recover the ethnic

awareness of Aymaran women that had cemented the new Federation. In this way ethnic and community organizations promoted
and underpinned the new unionism, so linking traditional and new
identities.

These experiences of community organization and political
struggle have the clear potential to create a new women's identity
that is quite different from the 'domestic female' or the 'political
man'. In their majority women were mobilized in workplace or
community organizations as a result of economic crisis (and
political repression), but the 'politics of needs' is also about
meaning and power (Escobar and Alvarez, 1992) and 'this crisis
mobilization has been truly transformative' (Chuchryk,
1989b:176). Women's experience of equality and community has
changed their sense of themselves and of their 'political' possibilities once and for all (Valenzuela, 1990). This means that mobilization around 'practical gender interests' may induce a greater
awareness of 'strategic interests' that are 'derived (deductively)
from an analysis of women's subordination and represent objectives which might overcome it' (Molyneaux, 1985:234).[13] But
this process is halting and contradictory, and the creation of a
new women's identity remains fractured and incomplete.

The kind of networking and community construction that
underpins the new identity is always crosscut by the clientelistic
relations that pervade local power structures. Not only are women
drawn into such relations, but their own organizations reproduce
them, so they do not remain immune to political manipulation
and personal jealousies and power struggles (Blondet, 1990).
Consequently there are 'manifold tendencies' amongst women's
organizations 'that do not derive mechanistically from the class or
racial status of their participants', so that adjacent urban communities may have very different demands and different ways of
getting them satisfied. These findings should caution us against
making blanket assertions about "Latin American women" and
"their interests" ' (Alvarez, 1990:266). Even where women have
grown more aware of their strategic interests it is unlikely these
will be 'universally endorsed' because they 'may threaten shorter-
term practical interests' (Molyneaux, 1985:234) such as the kind
of security or protection afforded by clientelism and paternalism.
Finally, amongst feminists themselves there have been enduring
ideological divisions between the 'historical' and mainly middle-
class feminists, the women from the urban movements, and the
combatants of national liberation struggles (Sternbach et al.,
1992). Moreover, many women's groups within the popular
church or traditional left were discouraged both from using the
feminist label and from pursuing such key issues of the feminist
agenda as sexual self-determination, abortion rights, and violence

against women. Some groups capitulated for fear of losing mass support or offending male comrades. Others began to think through their critique of male left politics, and called for a 'revolution in daily life' (Sternbach et al., 1992).

Feminism in Latin America has tended to receive a bad academic press. It has been seen as right-wing, especially in Chile where *El Poder Feminino* (Female Power) contributed to Allende's downfall,[14] and where electoral results had revealed that 'the vast majority of women oppose or are hostile towards social and collective emancipation' (Kirkwood, 1983:626). It has also been seen (sometimes in explicit comparison with women's role in urban social movements) as a small, upper-middle-class movement aping the manners of the North American sisters. In fact, it is now a 'thriving, broad-based movement' (Sternbach et al., 1992:394) that made a significant contribution to popular struggle under authoritarian regimes in Peru, Chile and Brazil. By 1983 in Chile the Movement for Women's Emancipation (MEMCH-83) brought together 24 of the huge range of women's organizations, while Women for Life emerged as the principal axis of female mobilization overall (Valenzuela, 1990). In Brazil the issues of 'militant motherhood' had driven the Female Amnesty Movement, the Cost of Living Movement and the Day Care Movement throughout the 1970s into the 1980s, and by 1985 'tens of thousands of women had been politicized by the women's movements, and core items of the feminist agenda had made their way into the platforms and programs of all major political parties' (Alvarez, 1989:18).

But the movements in Brazil and Chile were likely to have been exceptional, and not only for their militancy but also for their social scope. In Chile, the Feminist Movement managed to transcend its middle class origins and reach out to the poor women of the urban periphery (Valenzuela, 1990). In Brazil, 'the politicization of gender within Church-linked community women's groups provided nascent Brazilian feminism with an extensive mass base' (Alvarez, 1989:36), and 'feminists embraced the survival struggles of poor and working-class women and joined forces with the militant opposition' (Alvarez, 1990:265). This meant that in both countries new feminist groups proliferated and dozens of new neighbourhood women's organizations grew up on the urban peripheries; and in Brazil, especially, women of all classes were advancing a profusion of gender claims, with women's struggles being waged in factories, homes, community groups, parishes, legislatures and courts (Alvarez, 1990). In this way, feminist struggles began to intersect both with the survival struggles of the urban poor and with the democratic struggles of the political opposition to the military regimes.

There is no reason to doubt the political commitment of feminists to working class women or the poor women of the urban periphery. But the *theoretical* literature systematically fails to address the ways in which the women's movement, and women's mobilization in general, intersects with class, community or professional interests. In other words, it is assumed that wherever and however women mobilize they do so as women, and not as the urban poor, or as workers, teachers or students. (This assumption may be further reduced to the axiom that all movements that mobilize women must sooner or later discover the same goals and establish the same agenda.) This assumption returns us to the competing claims of class analysis and social movement theory with which the chapter began and which must remain unresolved so long as social identity is understood to be singular. But social identity, even or especially at individual level, is in fact multiple, and people are motivated to mobilize as women and teachers, as Indians and peasants, as students and democrats, as workers and socialists, or as any other more or less complex multiple identity. Therefore the construction of *collective* identity as a precondition or an integral part of successful social mobilization does not only have to do with the appeal to a priori interests, but to movement goals and a convincing strategy for achieving those goals. Social identity is both multiple and malleable, and is shaped not only by social context but also by institutional context and the strategic moment of engagement with the political world. These are topics for the next chapter.

4 The Politics of Social Movements

The Political Scope of Social Movements

The contemporary sociology of social movements tends to confine their activity to civil society and to constrain their political objectives. Social movements can recruit new members, take on new issues, debate new ideas and build new coalitions (Munck, n.d.), but the result is the 'restricted identity' (Zermeño, 1987) of a 'self-limiting radicalism' that is 'not necessarily or primarily oriented to the state' (Cohen and Arato, 1992:493). Habermas locates social movements in the socio-cultural sphere, where they contest creeping 'colonization' (Habermas, 1987). In similar vein, Touraine suggests that social movements are defending civil society against an all-consuming and technocratic state (Scott, 1991:66), while Melucci sees social movements embroiled in symbolic struggles where the stakes are increasingly zero-sum (Melucci, 1989). Social movements can therefore expand civil society or the public realm, but only through the kind of cultural innovations (Melucci, 1989) which are achieved outside of the political system (Touraine, 1988). Social movements involve struggles within civil society, remaining unconnected to state institutions and unconcerned with political parties (Scott, 1991:73). Social action is not strategic.

Such 'self-limiting' social movements are said to act in defense of their 'autonomy', meaning their autonomy from the state. This assertion becomes central in the Latin American context, where the presence of the state is often so overwhelming (see Chapter 2). Here the 'novelty' of the movements has been gauged by the 'extent to which they are independent of the state apparatus ... (and) untainted by official patronage' (Lehmann, 1990:151). Similarly their 'self-limiting' character is demonstrated by the gradual exclusion of important but prickly issues like land reform from their political agendas. Finally, following the European theorists, their potential for change is derived from their 'counter-cultural' and predominantly apolitical character (Evers, 1985). But it is a mistake to take the anti-statist rhetoric of social movements at its face value, and outside of its historical context. In Latin America, at least, the defense of 'autonomy' is often an attempt to distance contemporary movements from the political manipulation of the populist period (Moises, 1982; Assies et al., 1991); and the notion of autonomy (and its family of identity, authenticity and community) serves more general ideological purposes. On the one hand, social movements which are riven by factionalism and personal power struggles are presented as uncontaminated by 'politics'. On the other, movements may enjoy the (temporary) illusion that they can progress by ignoring the unequal power relations of their political environment. On both counts it is likely to be social movement leaders who speak of 'autonomy' while searching for political solutions.

In fact, contrary to the 'sociological' view, it appears that social movements are inevitably political, and must develop a political project if they are to prosper. First, they are political in the sense of politicizing new issues, and so express 'not a retreat from the political sphere, but an extension of politics to cover a wider range of concerns and social relations' (Scott, 1991:24). Secondly, they are political in the sense of entering the political and institutional arena, and of engaging in strategic interaction with the state. Hence, social movements are not 'social' because they are born of or belong to civil society. This view has been criticized for its 'underspecification of the institutional structures within which movements emerge and of the intermediate processes that turn structural potentials into collective action' (Tarrow, 1991:13). Nor are they 'social' because they eschew political demands. The labour movement, as much as the women's movement, came to press for political rights and an extension of the franchise, so demonstrating their direct concern with citizenship and political representation. But these movements may be social, insofar as they seek to link private concerns and pursuits with institutional and state sanctioned politics, and to construct an 'intermediate sphere' at the interface between state and civil society (Scott, 1991).

Scott defends his own thesis that 'social movements can be viewed as a reaction to the failure of the institutions of interest intermediation: parliaments, the media and especially political parties' (Scott, 1991:140). But social movement theory in general has moved from a predominant preoccupation with culture and collective identity to a closer focus on the relationships between movements and their political systems. These relationships are always interactive, and constructed on a specific legal and institutional terrain which is the accumulated historical result of both popular strategy and state policy (Foweraker, 1989a; 1993). Since no form of politics, however popular, can occur in a political and institutional vacuum, social movements have little choice about setting out across this terrain, but their choices multiply once they are there. For this is a strategic terrain where social movements find the legal and institutional means to negotiate with the state. Far from being a zero-sum game, by definition, the politics of social movements is a politics of incremental advance and disguised retreat, of frequent failures and partial successes.

These observations have been far from obvious in the Latin American context. Mainwaring and Viola contrasted the negotiable demands of interest groups with the non-negotiable demands of 'relatively apolitical' social movements (1984:20); and many accounts have tended to see Latin American social movements in terms of open confrontation with the state. Since these movements were often understood as the social response to authoritarian, repressive and incompetent regimes, this is not perhaps surprising. But the greatest number of studies concern social movements in Mexico, Peru and Brazil, where sprawling but centralized state administrations offered ample opportunities for negotiation and dialogue with a range of more or less sophisticated state apparatuses and agencies (Cardoso, 1983). And despite the apparent 'hostility towards formal politics' it gradually became clear that 'the movements tend frequently to rely on the state or other outside sources of material support' (Lehmann, 1990:174). It is true that such support only comes at a price; and that negotiation with the state has to be conducted in a context that may and often does include clientelism, patrimonialism, corruption and electoral fraud. But the frequent fact of negotiation does place the claim to autonomy in a different light. Autonomy is not the absence of political linkage, but a precondition of negotiation. And not each and every partial response to social movement demands is tantamount to cooptation. Partial successes and temporary reversals compose key aspects of the collective memory of struggle, and so reinforce social identity.

Linkages Between Social Movements and Political Systems

Explicating the linkages between social movements and the political system requires a dual focus: social movements are shaped by their political and institutional context as well as shaping that context in some degree. In the Latin American context, it is not difficult to demonstrate that the strength of social movements often turns on their success in negotiating with the state, but scant attention is paid to the way identity is constructed through interaction with the state, and this impedes a proper inquiry into social movement strategy (see Chapter 2). Indeed, the Latin American literature is heavily influenced by the rather idealized view of the macro-level of 'European' sociology, while ignoring the more realist approach of resource mobilization theory (Scott, 1991:113).[1] In the latter perspective, social movements have to overcome the problems of social action through increasing organization, and consequently have to increase their available resources by adopting lower-risk and more 'institutional' forms of action (Oberschall, 1973). The state becomes the central focus of movement strategy and state institutions come to shape movement trajectory. In particular, the recognition that movement leaders strive to win greater influence within the 'system' (and so secure their own position and prestige) is an effective check to naive notions of 'apolitical' movements. Elsewhere I have characterized these tendencies as the 'inevitable institutionalism' of Latin American social movements (Foweraker, 1993: ch. 10).

If social movements in Latin America have some impact on their political and institutional context, it is because they struggle to participate in their political systems (Touraine, 1987).[2] Theirs is not a struggle over 'historicity' (Touraine, 1988), nor a 'politics of influence ... aimed at intermediate structures of political society' (Cohen and Arato, 1992:561), but a struggle to integrate previously excluded groups and issues into local or national politics. These movements, therefore, do not differ in any essential way from 'normal' or 'institutionalized' forms of collective action, and are not irrational, non-strategic or 'autonomous' (Scott, 1991). On the contrary, they are not only strategic actors but also strongly 'institutionalist' in their strategic orientation.

In one view, social movements fail once they have been induced by institutional or other means to change from 'protest' to 'politics'. In the North American context, Piven and Cloward argue that once the movements have been drawn into 'normal' political channels, they can no longer be politically effective. The state responds to social mobilization by 'extending established procedures to new groups or new institutional arenas', and protesters win only 'what historical circumstances had already made ready to be conceded' (Piven and Cloward, 1977:33–6). In the Latin American context there are recurrent warnings and demonstrations of the dangers of cooptation by state agencies. But there is no compelling case for making political change and political integration (or cooptation) mutually exclusive. The process of integrating excluded groups into the political system is surely a process of political change and occasional reform; and the success of a social movement can be compatible (if not necessarily so) with its absorption and consequent decline. This argument has been applied to the Greens' entry into mainstream politics in Germany, and may apply a fortiori to the role of social movements in recent democratic transitions in Latin America (see Chapter 5).

State Influence on Social Movements

It is now recognized that the political and institutional context conditions the emergence, identity, organizational forms, strategy and overall trajectory of social movements. In Latin America this context is mainly comprised of the state in its many manifestations, but it will also include political parties, public administration, previous protest movements, as well as 'national political traditions and alignments' in general (Piven and Cloward, 1977:23). In some cases the rise of social movements is a direct response to state attempts to exclude large sectors of the population from social benefits or political participation. The remarkably stable political regimes of Colombia and Mexico, for example, have practised systematic and sometimes violent segregation of many popular sectors (while coopting the middle classes and privileged popular organizations, especially trade unions) (Touraine, 1987); and the military regime in Chile worked to 'suppress systems of broad representation' and to 'transfer basic state functions to market mechanisms', so that demands for wages, health care, social security and housing lost 'their traditional state referent' (Garretón, 1989:142). But all these countries experienced a dramatic expansion of social movement activity during the 1980s.

The politics of exclusion is premised on a parallel politics of (partial) inclusion, and the state in Latin America has traditionally acted to coopt social movements, mainly through corporatist mechanisms. Moreover, as suggested above, social movements often make demands which, if successful, entail some form of state intervention and regulation (Boschi, 1990); and even in the absence of active intervention the state can offer the kind of 'symbolic reassurance' that can dampen social protest (Tilly, 1978; 1979). The reforming military government in Peru (1968–75) successfully coopted urban social movements in Lima by setting up parallel organizations, bringing neighbourhood associations into public administration, and sponsoring self-help housing. Large organizations like the National System of Social Mobilization (SINAMOS) and the National Office of Young Settlements (ONDEPJOV) concentrated the clientelistic relations which tied popular energies to state purposes. And although the urban movements began to escape state control in subsequent years, the democratic government of Alan García again tried to coopt them on to government urban development programmes. Similarly ambitious schemes characterized the Chilean government's attempt to capitalize on the success of Female Power, the movement of middle-class women who had mobilized against Allende, and the threat of communism. By

1983 there were some 10,000 Mothers' Centres (CEMAs), under the leadership of Pinochet's wife, with around 230,000 members.

It is clear that in Latin America corporatist initiatives can encompass much broader sectors than the organized working class. In the European context, on the other hand, it is alleged that the prevalence of neocorporatist forms of representation has provoked the rise of social movements. The closed corporatist circuit continues to include labour organizations that are declining in importance because of macroeconomic changes, while excluding the dynamic middle classes within the expanding service sector (Scott, 1991). At the same time, the elitism, hierarchy and centralism of corporatist institutions have tended to dismiss grassroots demands, and displace conflict into social mobilization on the streets (Wilson, 1990). In short, the inclusionary mechanisms of neocorporatism effectively exclude new issues and new publics, and so serve to elicit what they are designed to suppress. Social movements seek to bring about change by 'opposing specific forms of social closure and exclusion' (Scott, 1991:150).

Such paradoxical effects are also apparent in Latin America, where the state itself has often promoted social mobilization, wittingly or unwittingly. In Brazil the social policies of the 'developmentalist' state, however inadequate in scope and delivery, created the kind of expectations and demands that precipitated social movements (Cardoso, 1983; Scherer-Warren and Krische, 1987). This was true of many urban popular movements, such as those based in the associations of slum-dwellers in Rio de Janeiro (Boschi, 1987), as well as rural movements that responded to the state's delegation of social protection programmes to rural unions (Keck, 1989; Maybury-Lewis, 1991). In this way, changes in the policies and culture of public administration could spawn new movements and new popular combativeness, while state manipulation of inflation figures provoked the Wage Recovery Campaign, with the Metalworkers Union of São Paulo in its vanguard. In Peru many of the land invasions on the urban periphery of Lima have been promoted by the state, either for speculative purposes or for the political purpose of building new clienteles (Castells, 1982). These same neighbourhoods were later mobilized again by the military regime, with popular organizations recurrently breaking free of clientelistic control. In the countryside too, both in Peru and Colombia, social movements emerged in the wake of the state's efforts to organize the peasantry within corporatist structures (Davis, 1989); and where the state then failed to respond to more independent demands there were outbreaks of guerrilla insurgency.[3]

Social movements arise in specific places at specific times for all sorts of reasons, but it is characteristic of many movements that 'their future members are unified by ... (their) common position in the same institutional context' (Tarrow, 1988b:283), and this is because 'institutional life aggregates people ... molds group identities, and draws people into the settings within which collective action can erupt' (Piven and Cloward, 1977:21). For this reason it is corporatist initiatives, above all, that prove most capable, directly or indirectly, of promoting social mobilization in Latin America. Within the institutional context the socially embedded actor (Morris and Mueller, 1992) can construct grievances, explore opportunities and generate resources. As such, the institutional setting is one specific form of 'micromobilization context' (see Chapter 2), [4] and it is important that 'institutions not only provide insurgents with causes for insurgency, (but) also make available the resources – economic, organizational and ideological – that permit them to turn anger and deprivation into mobilization' (Tarrow, 1988b:283). With its emphasis on individual and rational actors (and its preoccupation with social movement organizations), resource mobilization theory tends to ignore collective action within institutions, but Tilly (1984:312) is adamant that social movements can emerge within churches, schools, firms, and labour unions, as well as within national states. In Latin America both the Church and official (and corporatist) labour organizations have proved fecund institutional contexts for seeding social mobilization; and the movements that grow within them have often been adept at turning the solidarities and symbolism of the institution against itself.

But social movements derive not only from a setting of solidarity but also from a shared antagonism towards 'others', and so have been defined as a 'continuing overt relationship of conflict between collective actors and authorities' (Tarrow, 1988b:283). In particular, 'it is typically by rebelling against the rules and authorities associated with their everyday activities that people protest' (Piven and Cloward, 1977:21), because it is here that they are most likely to feel a sense of injustice or 'moral outrage' (Moore, 1973). The 'collective action frames' (Snow et al., 1986) that affirm people's commitment to the cause must therefore discover injustice and especially unjust authority if they are to be effective (Gamson, 1992), and recurrent conflict cements this solidary sense of identity and common cause (Thompson, 1974). This 'unjust' authority is nearly always vested in the state, because 'states hold an exceptional power to define actors in any arena as legitimate or illegitimate, hence to support some actors and destroy others'

(Tilly, 1984:312). In short, the state defines the rules and, although it may create the institutional contexts that foster social movements, it can also suppress them once they emerge. The relationship of social movements to the state is therefore very different from that of interest groups, especially in Latin America where movements routinely undergo state repression and violence. Over the past 20 years, Mexico's political regime has been more restrained than many across the continent, and it has kept social control largely through well tested forms of cooptation and clientelism. Nonetheless, the Mexican state has tended to lay siege to the more recalcitrant movements in both town and countryside, and has not hesitated to use violence to intimidate or disperse their members (Foweraker and Craig, 1990; Foweraker, 1993). During the same 20 years the intransigence and violence of many state apparatuses has triggered armed uprisings and guerrilla movements in Guatemala, Salvador, Nicaragua, Colombia, Peru, Brazil, Uruguay, Argentina and Mexico itself.

Yet the relationship between state and social movements in Latin America does not usually reach these extremes. The state is indeed the priority 'target' of many movements, but is often successful in dividing and disarticulating them before they pose any direct threat. Since social movements are often competing for the same scarce resources, the state responds selectively to their demands, so separating them and even setting them one against the other (Cardoso, 1983); while its services are granted as clientelistic favours, not as rights, so denying any unifying principle of entitlement (Mainwaring, 1987).[5] At the same time the state is not monolithic but a complex ensemble of different agencies, each with their own 'partial policies' (Cardoso, 1983) and distinctive modes of negotiation that will change from one political moment to the next. There are 'proper channels', but these remain obscure. There are schedules but 'bureaucratic time' varies across agencies and according to the requirements of political control (Telles, 1987). Moreover, since 'grassroots movements deal principally with the State at its most decentralized level – the specific organs of a given municipality – the "State" which one particular movement faces may differ substantially from the "State" which another one faces' (Mainwaring, 1989:169). Alliances between movements are therefore more difficult to achieve, and the experience of one movement will not easily serve the purposes of another. Hence most movements approach the state with some trepidation as they traverse this constantly shifting and deeply ambiguous legal and institutional terrain.

The Institutional Context of Social Mobilization

State efforts to control, channel, repress or facilitate social movements mean that 'collective action now assumes a more specifically political guise inasmuch as it constitutes itself against a power which it undermines or from which it attempts to extract concessions. Collective mobilization is therefore in itself laden with a political dimension, for it is formed in response to the state which it confronts' (Birnbaum, 1988:29). But the relationship between social movements and the state is not one of exteriority, with social actors gazing across barren terrain at the shining citadel on the hill. On the contrary, 'the forms of political protest ... are determined by the institutional context in which people live and work' (Piven and Cloward, 1977:14), and this context then 'provides a constitutive basis for collective action' (Rucht, 1990). This is what Giddens (1976) calls the 'duality of structure', and it is an insight that he has since developed in his theories of 'structuration'. Moreover, it is not just institutional constraints and legal protocols which operate in this way. 'Just as political leaders play an influential role in stimulating mass arousal, so do they play an important role in shaping the demands of the aroused' (Piven and Cloward, 1977:17).[6] These observations apply across the board to peasant movements, urban squatter movements or Catholic base communities: grassroots movements may be driven by material need and perceptions of social justice, but they are always configured in some degree by 'national patterns of power' (Eckstein, 1989). This does not mean that social movements are simply passive or 'supporting' actors on the political stage. On the contrary (as argued in the following sections), since 'the state tends generally to be the favourite target of a social movement' it always develops the kind of dynamism that 'gives rise to many shifting strategies on the part of all actors involved' (Birnbaum, 1988:32). In short, all social movements must be defined in some degree by their political projects, or their attempts to influence institutional and political change.[7]

In approaching the state or developing a political project it is a commonplace observation that social movements become 'institutionalized'. This occurs to the degree that they enter 'conventional politics' (Tarrow, 1988a:427) or achieve some degree of representation (which may serve to mitigate the impact of direct participation). In short, institutionalization occurs at the 'mesolevel' of collective action and this is the key to understanding the phenomenon (McAdam et al., 1988). This mesolevel includes a kaleidescope of 'mesostructural factors' like pre-existing organizations, party constellations, rules and policies, public opinion, and even factions internal to the movement itself (Rucht, 1990). Thus, just as movements emerge in 'micromobilization contexts' which disseminate 'ideological frames', so are they institutionalized through the decline of mass mobilization and the distribution of selective incentives, the cooptation of leaders into established institutions, and the efforts of political parties and interest groups to adapt to the insurgency and absorb its energy (Tarrow, 1990). Hence, 'institutionalization must be thought of as an inherent part of the logic of collective action since it is instrumental in producing the rhythmic ebb and flow seen in the formation of collectivities' (Boschi, 1987:183).

The tendency towards institutionalization will inevitably create tensions in grassroots movements which practice different forms of direct democracy; and radical theorists like Castells and Touraine are suspicious that organization and formal leadership structures may invite symbolic responses and consequent demobilization. More concretely it is alleged that protest is 'inhibited by constraints that result from the vertical integration upon which the organizational maintenance by relatively resourceless groups often depends' (Piven and Cloward, 1992). In short, to pretend that an approximation to 'conventional politics' is without its costs is 'to trivialize the realities of power'. But others argue that social movements are condemned to sterility if they do not develop Social Movement Organizations (SMOs) to assume the executive functions previously exercised by informal groups, and to carry out 'the crucial task of mediating between the larger macro environment and the set of micro dynamics on which the movement depends' (McAdam et al., 1988). Part and parcel of this process will be the professionalization of the intellectuals who must synthesize the philosophy and goals of the movement for consumption by the mass media (Eyerman and Jamison, 1991). The trajectory of the movement itself will then depend on how successfully its SMO negotiates the complexities of the legal and institutional terrain linking the movement to the state. The presence of countermovements and competing SMOs further complicates the terrain, and, although ad hoc alliances are sometimes achieved, enduring coalitions between SMOs remain rare. Finally, the success of SMO initiatives also depend on its specific context: does it face a democratic or authoritarian regime? And where does its struggle fall within the overall 'cycle of protest'?

In general, the form of state which collective action confronts will have a crucial influence on the form and content of the action because 'the particular logic of each state imposes itself on all the social actors involved ... (who are) forced to adopt modes of behaviour which correspond to the kind of state they are facing' (Birnbaum 1988:32). Commenting on Tilly's detailed studies of social mobilization in France, Birnbaum suggests that 'in a somewhat paradoxical manner, the power of the state gives rise to a significant mobilization against it, which in turn provokes a further strengthening of the state, and not, so far, its disappearance'. This kind of interaction recalls the rise of social movements under authoritarian regimes in Latin America, and Birnbaum could certainly have these cases in mind when he concludes that 'mobilizations themselves seem to be more frequent, more widespread and more violent in such bureaucratic societies' (Birnbaum, 1988:190).

The particular form of state that confronts social movements comes to create a specific 'system of opportunities and constraints' (Melucci, 1988:332) that the theory now designates as a 'political opportunity structure' (POS). With the emergence of the national state social movements themselves become potentially national in scope, and the POS then becomes central to social movement activity which 'corresponds to the process by which a national political system shapes, checks, and absorbs the challenges which come to it' (Tilly, 1984:312). The notion of the POS was first mooted, implicitly, by Lipsky (1968) before being elaborated to include the degree of openness or closure of the polity; the stability of political alignments; the presence or absence of allies; divisions within the elite or its tolerance of protest, and policy-making innovations by government itself (Tarrow, 1988a:429). It is now used to explain both cross-national variations in social movement trajectories and the 'receptivity or vulnerability of the political system to organized protest' (McAdam et al., 1988). But a unique emphasis on the POS may obscure the difference between social movements and other collective actors like interest groups (Melucci, 1988), while the problem with applying the POS analytically is that it is not so much a variable as a cluster of variables, which may diverge significantly between democratic and authoritarian regimes (Tarrow, 1988a).

One of the few explicit applications of the POS to Latin America criticizes the notion as 'underspecified' and self-consciously addressed to the political systems of the industrialized democracies. Departing from a working definition of the POS as 'the configuration of forces in a (potential or actual) group's political environment that influences that group's assertion of its political claims' (Brockett, 1991:254), the study specifies its 'best-guess' variables of the POS as the presence or absence of allies, the availability of access points to the political system, the state's capacity and propensity for repression, elite fragmentation and conflict, and the temporal location of the movement itself in the 'cycle of protest' (see below). Having tailored the POS to the realities of authoritarian regimes the study then proceeds to apply it to peasant mobilization in Central America. Allies and especially outside organizers were important everywhere. Access to the political system was poorly institutionalized, especially for peasants, and so tended to fluctuate dramatically with a major impact on mobilization potentials. (Access improved rapidly in Nicaragua with the Revolution, as witnessed in the influence of the rural unions on the 1981 Agrarian Reform Law and the subsequent acceleration of land reform.) Repression was most widespread in Guatemala and Salvador, where it 'worked', and in Nicaragua, where it failed, partly because (on the elite conflict variable) the agrarian bourgeoisie of Nicaragua was never so cohesive as those of Salvador and Guatemala. (When the beginning of elite dissensus opened the way for a revolutionary uprising in Salvador in 1979/80, the US-backed government responded with state terror.) The final variable of location in the 'protest cycle' proved less important, precisely because all the states opted early for widespread repression, but, overall, the POS plays a useful analytical role in this comparative inquiry.

The POS also enters the theoretical account of the 'protest cycle' which begins with an historical cluster of movements in circumstances where grievances are generalized across sectors and worked into broader ideological and political projects (Tarrow, 1988b). Within the cycle, 'the magnitude of conflict, its social and geographical diffusion, the forms of action employed, and the number and types of SMOs involved vary in concert over time' (Tarrow, 1988a:433). The tactics, and therefore the rhythm of struggle, may be constrained by anchoring 'master frames' or advanced by the construction of a new frame (Snow and Benford, 1992:142), just as the civil rights movement in the United States in the 1960s created a 'rights frame' which benefited later struggles by Chicanos, gays and Native Americans. But the existence of a 'protest cycle' finally tends to suggest that it is not so much internal as environmental developments which do most to shape the trajectory of social movements, and that such cycles express the collective responses of citizens, groups and elites to 'an expanding structure of political opportunities' (Tarrow, 1991:13). At the same time the cycle creates its own 'environment' so that 'groups which emerge on the crest of a wave of protest may profit from the general atmosphere of discontent created by the efforts of others' (Tarrow, 1988a:433). The rise and decline of these cycles can only be explained at the intersection between movements and the POS in particular forms of state; but, Tarrow warns, 'theories of the state carry the risk of surveying the terrain of collective action from so high an altitude that crucial processes and internal variations cannot be seen' (Tarrow, 1988a:436).

On the basis of his study of Central American peasant movements Brockett concludes that the location of social movements in the 'protest cycle' cannot be very important 'in systems where both meaningful popular access to the political system and the rule of law are not institutionalized ... (and where) elites are still able to end popular mobilization through widespread repression when the level of protest too seriously threatens their interests' (Brockett, 1991:267). But there appears to be strong prima facie evidence of such cycles in the popular protests against authoritarian regimes in Latin America, and especially in Brazil (1977–84), Chile (1983–9) and Mexico (1985–8). In these cases not only does the amount of mobilization increase as the wave of protest builds up, but the POS also expands through processes of liberalization (Brazil), constitutional referendum (Chile) and electoral participation (Mexico). The wave is set off by small vanguards or 'exemplary individuals' (O'Donnell and Schmitter, 1986: ch. 3), but the strength of the ground swell startles movement leaders who have not seen beyond their own particular concerns. Indeed, since most movements are motivated by their own specific needs and demands, a 'master frame' must emerge to link them together and set the agenda for future movement activity and regime responses. In Mexico the rapid entry of social movements into the electoral arena encourages a renewed demand for 'effective suffrage'; in Brazil the rising cycle culminates in the demand for 'Direct Elections, Now'; in Chile the different movements gradually coalesce around an undifferentiated demand for democracy (summed in a single syllable – No – at the moment of the referendum). Such cycles may end through attrition and repression (Mexico), or through exhaustion and factionalism both between and within movements (Brazil) (O'Donnell and Schmitter, 1986:26), or because the movements' objectives have been won (Chile). The nature of the demands, the strategy of the social movements and the configuration of the POS will all contribute to determine the outcome of the cycle.

The notion of the POS is both objective and subjective. It describes a real configuration of laws, institutions and policies, but suggests that social movements must first perceive the 'system of constraints and opportunities' before acting upon it. But the state policies of authoritarian regimes in Latin America clearly sharpened such perceptions, often in repressive and violent ways. This can be illustrated by returning to the redefinition of the division between public and private by a new generation of political women (see Chapter 3), and reviewing it from the perspective of state policy. In Brazil it was largely the economic policies of the 'developmentalist' state that destroyed poor families' survival strategies and pushed millions of women into the workforce, sometimes propelling them into community struggles; while the expansion of the state bureaucracy drew middle-class women into professional careers within public administration (Alvarez, 1990). In Chile the threat to economic survival was just as great and the changes in women's economic roles just as radical, but the experience of dictatorship also taught that 'authoritarianism pervades the entire social structure' (Kirkwood, 1983:635). The state (especially in Chile and Argentina) set out to suppress all conventional channels of political representation and so suffocate the public sphere. But in attempting to 'privatize' political life it effectively politicized private life (Oszlak, 1987), and this had 'an important impact on redefinitions of the relation between the public and private spheres' (Jelin, 1990:3). Thus it was the combination of economic policy and political repression that wrought the changes, mainly because 'in the case of Latin American women ... the repressive state apparatus and the market encroach increasingly on private life, undermining traditional social organization' (Arizpe, 1990:xvii).

Traditionally the 'women's realm' had been 'the private sphere, which comprised religion, the family, relations with kinfolk and social dynamics'. This private sphere was especially important in ethnic communities because it was 'the space where indigenous language, identity and vision of the universe is protected' (Jelin, 1990:xviii), and so provided the conditions for 'ethnic defence'. But, although the authoritarian regimes of the 1970s and 1980s appealed to Christian family values and extolled women's traditional roles, state and market combined to destroy this 'lifeworld', while 'disappearances' and torture violated the sanctity of the family. Women quickly came to realize that these 'changes in the definition of what is the private and what is the public domain ... surpass by a long way the programmes for social transformation currently presented by most political parties' (Jelin, 1990:xviii); and, more importantly, that 'the institutionalized separation between public and private is constantly redefined ideologically and new definitions are coercively enforced by the State' (Alvarez, 1990:29). In other words, it is alleged that women came to a new perception of the state as a patriarchal state, with military authoritarianism the 'highest form' of patriarchal oppression. For this reason Latin American feminism became an 'intrinsically oppositional movement' (Sternbach et al., 1992) which confronted state power as the 'gendered' protection of a public domain of male politics. Insofar as this is true, it will certainly alter the women's movements' perception of the POS in any one country at any one time, with enduring consequences for their political strategies. This reinforces the observation that the 'newness' of contemporary social movements in Latin America may lie first and foremost in the new and different quality of their relationship to the state.

The Impact of Social Movements on the State

Early in the development of social movement theory in the United States, Lipsky had approached protest 'as a political process' which was 'increasingly directed toward government' (Lipsky, 1968:1154). He noted that movement leaders 'frame strategies according to their perception of the needs of (many) other actors' (Lipsky, 1968:1146), and recommended that research should focus on 'ways in which access to public officials is obtained by relatively powerless groups' (Lipsky, 1968:1158). A few years later Gamson (1975) insisted on the importance of political alliances and state action to the relative success of social movements; and Piven and Cloward (1977) also argued that it was institutional and political resources which made protest effective (Tarrow, 1988a). But the predominant resource mobilization paradigm was slow to address the political dimension of social protest, and the preferred research tool of political scientists, the survey, failed to discover or measure the impact of social movements on their political environment. But after an encounter with European theory, and several years' reflection, it was finally concluded that 'the dynamics of collective action – even in its most 'expressive' and anti-political forms – are best understood in relation to the political process' (Tarrow, 1988a:422).

Perspectives were also changing in Europe. The most cogent original argument in defence of the non-institutional character of social movements had come from Claus Offe (1985), who now suggested that successful mobilization could only be maintained if the political pressure it created was channelled into 'dominant political institutions' (Kitschelt, 1990:243). This required a strategic 'self-transformation' because an instrumental approach to state institutions differs from a more 'expressive' identity orientation, and entails a different 'action repertoire'. In place of subcultural retreat or countercultural challenge a more institutionalist strategy would require participation, negotiation, pressure and confrontation. Theorists like Melucci criticized the 'political reductionism' or 'myopia of the visible' which focused uniquely on the 'measurable aspects of the collective action (confrontation with the political system and effects on policies) and ignored the production of new cultural codes' which are the precondition for such visible action (Melucci, 1988:334), while 'fundamentalists' within the movements themselves resisted the strategic switch to public policy objectives. But most theorists now recognized that 'every movement has a visible and a latent reality' (Rucht, 1990:164), and social movements began to practise a 'politics of influence' which is 'specifically suited to modern civil societies whose public spheres, rights and representative democratic institutions are, in principle at least, open to discursive processes that inform, thematize and potentially alter social norms and political cultures' (Cohen and Arato, 1992:504).

In Latin America it was the Leninist and military left which was first predominant in opposition to the authoritarian regimes of the recent period; but its failure to generate popular support, and its final defeat, led to a profound re-evaluation of the strategic orientation of popular politics. Subsequently, social movements arose to press popular demands on the state, but recent assessments of their political impact are often pessimistic. There are many of them, but they are isolated, ideologically and politically (and this leaves them open to repression). The process of identity formation is often conflictual, with unity the exception rather than the rule. Linkages to state institutions are precarious and many movements, especially urban movements, are defensive in nature, seeking to protect their small patrimony rather than taking new demands to the state (Mainwaring, 1987). Much of this scepticism regarding the political potential of the movements is simply a readjustment after the heady utopianism of the 1970s, when urban social movements especially were seen as a popular panacea (Assies et al., 1991). At the same time, the scepticism may reflect a simple misconception of the proper and possible role of the movements. Their strength and political importance derive from a growing capacity to negotiate with the state, not from any tendency to direct action against the government or its agencies. In short, 'most social movements do not represent regime challenges; their goals are far more limited' (McAdam et al., 1988:721).

Social movements in Latin America have shown 'a consistent disposition to negotiate' with the state (Boschi, 1987a), and a large part of their political practice is devoted to developing an effective *capacidad de gestión*, loosely translated as the ability to get things done, or get demands met (Foweraker and Craig, 1990). Boschi demonstrated that urban associations in Brazil, for example, were continually involved with public agencies, especially in cases of land invasion or property seizure where the outcome was intimately related to the state's response. By 1982 there were 8,000 such associations across the country, many enjoying some form of local or regional government patronage, or some form of support from political parties. Most mobilization by these associations aims to provide, or to get government to provide, basic urban services such as electricity, paved roads, sewage systems, water supplies, bus routes, schools, medical posts and so on. Inevitably social movements must compete amongst themselves for state resources, and have no choice but to go 'rent-seeking in the hope of achieving something, however small and for however few people, or opting out entirely of political pressure politics – which amounts to leaving others to collect the rents' (Lehmann, 1990:152). But such rents, or piecemeal welfarism, usually come at a price, and the state can attach political conditions to the selective provision of scarce resources. In this way social movements can fast lose sight of their 'autonomy' inside the machinations of municipal or regional politics. Two competing slum-dwellers' organizations emerged in Rio de Janeiro in the late 1970s, one linked to a left-wing party and the other to the conservative state governor.

This political involvement by social movements will certainly hasten their 'institutionalization', but the political practices and policy outputs of state institutions are changing too. By engaging with municipal politics, urban social movements have had some success in pressing the state to fulfil its legal and normative obligations of guaranteeing individual security, protecting the property of the poor from fraud and violence, and enforcing its own rules, regulations, and price controls. Far from the urban centres, in the heartland of the Amazon region, other movements have successfully defended rubber-tapping areas and fought flooding by major dam projects. Thus, although contemporary movements may appear similar to popular organizations of yesteryear, only an 'ingenuous historicism' (Melucci, 1988) will deny the novelty of their political practices and especially of their relationship with the state. Nonetheless, it is altogether too wishful to suggest that *across the continent* social movements are beginning to move from the micro to the macro level, and from 'protest to proposal' (Fals Borda, 1992).

Social Movements and the Legal–Institutional Terrain

In attempting to explain the emergence of social movements, the theory has returned recurrently to the mediations between objective circumstance and collective action. But once such action is underway the focus of attention shifts to the problem of accounting for its political impact and outcomes. A variety of conceptual schemes has addressed this key question of how 'new collectivities can pressure their way into becoming legitimate political actors' (Boschi, 1987a:182). Tarrow talks of the 'political opportunity structure', Klandermans of the 'multiorganizational fields' (Klandermans, 1992), and Salman of the 'arena of confrontation' (Salman in Assies et al., 1991). With the possible exception of Salman, these different schemes all attempt to mix the institutional and legal boundaries of social movement activity with the presence of other social actors and social projects (whether rooted in the state or civil society or both); and it is unclear if the state is a privileged point of reference or not. My own notion of the 'legal and institutional terrain', on the other hand, is clearly state-centred and confined to institutions and legal and other rules of the game. Nonetheless, the terrain is not permanent but plastic, and changes its contours in response to state policy and social mobilization (Foweraker, 1989a; 1989b; 1993).

Social movements in Latin America have mainly sought material improvements for local communities, and the failure to obtain some kind of material response has nearly always led to demobilization. In developing this *capacidad de gestión* the movements have focused primarily on state organs and agencies, especially at the level of local government. In so doing they have increasingly sought some form of communitarian control of government policy and service provision, and most cross-class alliances between movements have had this goal (Davis, 1989:231). At the same time public administration, even at its most technical and bureaucratic, is porous at the edges, with areas of the state apparatus gradually becoming more receptive to popular participation and offering some support or succour to social movements, especially in the urban context (Cardoso, 1992). In this way some social movements can become 'valid interlocutors', in the vernacular, and begin to play significant roles in negotiating policy decisions and political outcomes. New links are forged between social movement leaders, party activists and state personnel. The political goals of the movements broaden. The movements themselves become politicized.

Contemporary social movements tend to insist on their autonomy, but their practice is more complex and contradictory than this suggests. The claim to autonomy is meant to vindicate present practice, and make it different from past participation in populist politics. Moises' study of the Societies of Friends of the Neighbourhood in Brazil suggests that the military authoritarian regime suppressed the traditional and clientelistic ties to 'the system', so obliging the urban social movements of the

1970s to seek new strategies and new forms of linkage (Moises, 1977). Similarly the new unionism which arose in São Paulo broke with *peleguismo* (corrupt control by state-owned union bosses) and initiated direct negotiations with employers. Implicit here is a greater sensitivity to the constraints and potential opportunities of the legal and institutional terrain, and some social movements now attempt to take advantage of political divisions within and between state agencies, and to seek out state personnel who are more disposed to respond to popular demands. Such tendencies become more accentuated during periods of liberalization (post 1974 in Brazil) or 'political opening' (the Echeverría administration in Mexico).[8] Moreover, in some cases, these piecemeal attempts to secure a political foothold in the state apparatus, and so derive some material advantage, have a broader political impact. Thus, state responses to the apparently restricted problem of popular housing in Brazil led to a general reorientation of political economy (Krischke, 1987). By pressing for more direct participation, and by seeking ways to influence public administration, social movements can begin to place new issues on the political agenda and to redefine 'the boundaries of institutional politics' (Dalton and Kuechler, 1990:298).

The resource mobilization theorists have downplayed direct power struggles between social movements and political authorities, and have stressed the mutual permeation and interpenetration of SMOs and state agencies. At the same time 'the decentralized, public, pluralist structure of civil society encourages efforts to influence sectors of public opinion, in this case the "conscience communities" or "social elites" ' (Cohen and Arato, 1992:506). But this 'politics of influence' appears peculiar to the United States (see Chapter 2), and even here it is objected that 'lower stratum protesters' only have 'some possibility of influence ... if their actions violate rules and disrupt the workings of an institution on which important groups depend' (Piven and Cloward, 1977:319). This comment applies a fortiori to Latin America where social movements have often had to engage in almost permanent mobilization, with recurrent confrontations, in order to achieve some degree of political connection without cooptation. And it is only mobilization that 'works'. Even in the Chile of the 1980s, something of a 'limiting case', mobilization won concessions: wage rises for the middle classes, changes in labour relations, the return of political exiles, the publication of opposition journals, and some small and discretionary degree of political 'opening' (Garretón, 1989b).

Mobilization is the main means available to social movements to press their demands. Hence the name. The rejection of demands may lead to demobilization, higher levels of mobilization, or different demands. Where social or economic demands are rejected, social movements will often turn their attention to the political conditions for putting their demands and getting them met (Foweraker, 1989a; 1993). The satisfaction of demands, on the other hand, can and often does spur further demands, as in the case of the women's movement from the suffragettes onwards. (This is another reason why the 'integration' or political absorption of a social movement does not necessarily spell failure.) The process of demand-making itself implies that social movements have acquired some 'sense of efficacy' and a belief that they can 'alter their lot' (Piven and Cloward, 1977), especially when demands are stated in terms of rights. From this critical moment the demands lose their quality of petition and reverberate with calls for change. From this moment too demands are directed straight to the state, since it alone is capable of delivering these rights (Caldeira, 1990:48). In this sense, social movements are more than mere survival strategies and must finally seek 'emancipation and a change of institutionalized norms, roles and rules' (Assies et al., 1991:89). Thus, 'the proper analogy to a social movement is neither a party nor a union but a political campaign. What we call a social movement consists in a series of demands or challenges to power-holders in the name of a social category that lacks an established political position' (Tilly, 1985:736).

In this connection it is clear that both the process of demand-making and the content of the demands are important to the description and explanation of social movement activity. In the European context, Scott suggests that social movements present two different orders of demand from two distinct social groups: on the one hand there are the groups excluded from social benefits (or 'social rights' in Marshall's language), and, on the other, there are the groups excluded from political decision-making (Scott, 1991:132). In Latin America too social movements tend to articulate two different sorts of demand, but these different demands cannot be attributed to distinct social groups. First are the material demands for economic distribution, public utilities or social benefits which initially motivate many of the movements. These are equivalent to Gramsci's 'economic corporate' demands and are rooted in sector, territory, community, union or firm. They represent demands for social inclusion and greater participation in the 'commonweal'. Although, in particular cases, they may reveal an 'uneasy fit between political structures and social demands' (Davis, 1992:411), and although they may compete with national development objectives (especially if based in specific regions or urban districts), they do not call for new rules or challenge the central norms of the political system overall. Secondly (but not necessarily 'later' in time) are demands for legal and political rights (habeas corpus, equality before the law, land rights, labour rights, voting rights) which together represent a claim to citizenship and so may indeed challenge the core values and operational codes of the system. In Latin America these different sorts of demand are not specific to particular social sectors or groups, but are often integral to the same, more or less continuous process of demand-making.

Yet the political effects of these distinct orders of demand can indeed by very different. The majority of 'economic corporate' demands can be easily absorbed or diverted within political systems organized along clientelistic and corporatist lines. Indeed, such systems are especially effective in separating and isolating this order of demand, and then providing partial satisfaction, and often ensuring cooptation, through granting (personal) favours and according (restricted) privileges. But since demands for citizenship rights always have a universal content (insofar as the rights must apply equally and across the board to be rights at all), they necessarily challenge the particularism of the clientelistic power relations that are so pervasive throughout the continent. It is alleged that in the European context struggles for the extension of citizenship are increasingly differentiated into new fields and new forms of action, and cannot therefore be imagined as 'collective actors moving on the historical stage like the characters of an epic drama' (Melucci, 1988:331). In Latin America, on the contrary, citizenship struggles still have universal content and universal scope, and, moreover, remain central to the political activity of social movements.

This struggle for citizenship rights can clearly be seen in the way the women's movements challenged the traditional boundaries between private and public; and may best be illustrated by the Mothers of the Plaza de Mayo who acted as an authentic Greek chorus in calling for retribution against the Argentine military regime. In this 'epic drama' their children and husbands were among the 20,000 people 'disappeared' by the regime, and every week they left their homes for the central square of Buenos Aires to challenge the military prohibition on public meetings, and so liberate their public space. Evidently women's mobilization of this kind is based on their traditional roles of reproduction and nurture, but this does not make it conservative. It may derive from the domestic sphere but it requires leaving that sphere. Conservative opinion would keep women's activity within neighbourhood associations and community organizations which are 'regarded as being an extension of the home' (Kirkwood,

1983:629), but domestic concerns take on radical implications in public space. A further example is São Paulo's massive nurseries campaign which soon made nurseries the kind of 'natural right' that clearly reversed traditional values for tens of thousands of women. In this way social movements can 'legitimate the politicization of the private sphere in defense of individual rights' (Alvarez, 1990:74), and bring women into the public sphere where their very presence automatically redefines the boundary between the private and the public, the personal and the political, the 'natural' and the 'artificial' (Alvarez, 1990:24). Like the Mothers their mobilization may be driven by an ethical imperative, or it may be driven by social need, but in either event it represents a far-reaching political challenge as witnessed in the 'horrifying acts of torture, sexual outrage and rape perpetrated against those women who have crossed the dividing line and entered that public sphere' (Kirkwood, 1983:631). Alvarez (1990) concludes that the public-private tension confers on women a special potential in the struggle for citizenship rights under authoritarian regimes.

It is suggested that in the early stages of authoritarian rule in Brazil 'most women's groups, like other opposition organizations in civil society, engaged exclusively in the politics of protest and in promoting critical consciousness and aiding grassroots survival efforts' (Alvarez, 1990:34). During this period the women sought 'absolute autonomy' from state-chartered political parties and state-controlled labour unions in order to avoid institutionalization or cooptation. But with the liberalization of the regime, the women's movements began to make gender-based claims on state and 'political society'. In this way the movements not only grew but also gained a strong degree of political recognition in both Brazil and Nicaragua, mounted a strong challenge to the regime in Chile, and joined struggles for national liberation in Salvador and, to a lesser degree, in Guatemala. And where the movements made most political impact and succeeded in developing a mass base (mainly in Brazil, Chile and Nicaragua), political parties and governments were keen to take up women's issues and so jump onto the 'pro-female' bandwagon (Sternbach et al., 1992:421).

The Influence of Political Parties on Social Movements

For some years social movement theory paid little attention to the 'institutional fabric in which movements are enmeshed' (Kitschelt, 1990). The resource mobilization approach, however, succeeded in demonstrating that 'far from being detached from traditional organizations of interest intermediation, they appear to be enmeshed in the socio-political networks of the societies in which they develop' (Klandermans, 1990:125). The crucial relationship here is that between social movements and political parties. In the European context it is often alleged that social movements respond to the failures of existing agencies of interest intermediation, and this may have impeded research into the links between movements and parties. One exception has been Kitschelt's research into the 'left-libertarian' parties which have a 'natural affinity' with social movements insofar as both are opposed to the institutional form and substance of the post-war class compromise (Kitschelt, 1990).

The Latin American literature recurrently recognizes the positive role played in social movements by 'outsiders' such as 'clergy, left wing parties, students, social workers, NGOs and lawyers, teachers and doctors' (Assies et al., 1991). The outsiders often hold the key to collective action, since they are able to advise on organization, the law and the political landscape, as well as supporting movements in their negotiations with political authorities. Most social movements will sooner or later need some kind of funding to pay for organizational costs, and some will finally seek political alliances to press their demands. In Mexico the *lideresas* who came to counsel women's organizations on the urban periphery helped integrate them into the 'welfare' system implicit in the local pattern of clientelistic power relations (Massolo and Ronner, 1983). In Rio de Janeiro 'without support from the Church and the Marxian left, neighbourhood movements have experienced considerable difficulty in developing, except in the face of a concrete threat from the outside, as in the case of *favela* removals or land expulsions' (Mainwaring, 1989:194). In short, an insistence on 'autonomy' does not mean that social movements automatically refuse outside assistance and advice.

Some believe that links with parties are especially important because 'political parties can offer social movements an opportunity to shape policy in a non-reactive manner' (Munck, n.d.). Yet this will clearly depend on what party in what place at what time, as Schneider demonstrates in her work on urban social movements in Chile (Schneider, 1992). The organizations linked to the Christian Democrat party were weakened by its ambivalence towards the dictatorship, while those linked to the socialists were hampered by their internal divisions. Yet the communist neighbourhoods maintained high levels of resistance throughout the Chilean 'cycle of protest', the Communist Party acting as 'the small motor that turned the larger motor of the mass movement'. This remained true so long as the communists continued to emphasize grassroots organization and the education of popular leaders. In Yungay, for example, the Party worked within the community together with the Church in a genuine exercise of popular democracy. But once Party activists began to organize cultural centres and human rights groups as political fronts for their own project, grassroots support declined; and the insurrectional strategy which the Party adopted after 1983 accelerated this process. By pulling its leaders out of the neighbourhood organizations the Party began to lose touch with its mass base, and its new militancy left it increasingly isolated.

In general it appears that political party activity is always potentially divisive of social movements at the local and community level in Latin America. Put most succinctly this is because 'joining a party breaks up the consensus created by common experience' (Cardoso, 1983:238), and so 'parties have generally reinforced the isolation and fragmentation of grassroots movements' (Mainwaring, 1987:147). Since social movements generally articulate 'economic corporate' demands of a sectoral, regional, or communal kind it is unlikely that their goals correspond to any particular party political platform (Nunes and Jacobi, 1983); while parties may find it difficult to incorporate the specific and often contradictory demands of social movements into their political programmes. Hence parties and movements may have partly complementary but finally competing agendas (Munck, n.d.). At the same time the movements may cling to notions of autonomy and direct participation, in contrast to the political party role of representation (Boschi, 1984). In addition to different agendas and different roles, the sad fact is that party militancy and divisions often exacerbate the factionalism which tends to infect social movements (Foweraker, 1993: ch. 6).

If parties are divisive in varying degrees throughout Latin America, they are especially so in Chile, where most urban squatter settlements have been organized by political parties for the past 30 years. Since these traditional actors channelled most demands for housing and services, a genuinely popular leadership failed to emerge, and since different settlements had different leaderships, the urban movement never achieved any kind of unity, but continued to align under separate political flags. 'Instead of being an instrument for re-establishing people's unity, the *pobladores'* movement amplified ideological cleavages' (Castells, 1982:269). This was still true during the first wave of protest in the 1980s (May 1983 to October 1984). These struggles remained largely uncoordinated because the political leaders who sought to ride the wave tended to 'parachute' into urban neighbourhoods, leaving little political residue other than political division and decay. (In the following year almost

35,000 people were arrested for political motives.) Later, when the parties had coalesced into broader alliances against the dictatorship, their different strategies and goals still had a visible demobilizing impact on popular organizations at the grassroots. Commentators agree that, if political clientelism is the bane of social movements in Brazil, so party divisions are their scourge in Chile (Garretón, 1989a; Lehmann, 1990).

The women's movement in Latin America has had an especially tense relationship with political parties, not least those of the left. Large numbers of women joined the political opposition in Peru, Argentina, Chile and Brazil, but the left-wing, political party organizations in these countries (and elsewhere) were committed to class struggle, not to women's liberation, and so women's issues were relegated to a poor second place. Radical women of early feminist beliefs (students, guerrillas, unionists, artists) found that they had to organize clandestinely, or see their struggles subsumed within male-dominated left politics. According to the leaders of the left, the women massed in hundreds of organizations in factories and poor urban districts across the continent were to form a 'rearguard' in support of the revolutionary project (Sternbach et al., 1992).

These problems were evident in Chile during the 'cycle of protest' of the 1980s. Women formed a clear majority within the organizations in defence of the family, and on behalf of the disappeared and the political prisoners, and together these organizations underpinned a powerful social movement. This movement had recourse to the proscribed political parties of the left in its search for political representation; but the left failed to recognize the movement, and tried to coopt and control the women's organizations for its own political purposes (Valenzuela, 1990). Moreover, the traditional left paid no attention to the 'seventy or eighty per cent of women who on all formal political occasions align themselves with the established order' (Kirkwood, 1983:629). Subsequently, as the political struggle took on a higher profile, the parties began to divide the women's organizations (and from 1984 many began to withdraw from their national coalitions (see Chapter 3)). The feminists continued to insist on the priority of women's issues, while the *políticas* were ready to pursue broader left-wing goals. Women who wanted both together opted for what they called 'double militancy' (Safa, 1990), but in fact 'double militancy' tended to weaken the women's agenda (Valenzuela, 1990). Nonetheless, the women of Chile did manage to mobilize jointly in both 1986 and 1988.

It was a similar story in Brazil, once opposition to the regime increased after 1980 and electoral competition sharpened. 'Old political and partisan divisions among movement participants were reopened, resulting in new forms of ideological struggle within the women's movement. (Moreover), as legal parties of the recently divided opposition scrambled to secure votes for the 1982 elections, there was renewed partisan struggle over the organized constituencies and mobilizational potential of the feminist and feminine movements' (Alvarez, 1989:45). Alvarez notes that many of these divisions were not strictly partisan but rather reflected differences over strategy or personal rivalries and power struggles. Nonetheless many women's organizations broke apart under these strains, although tensions tended to be less acute within social movements on the urban periphery, and feminism *qua* social movement began to give way to the interest-group strategies of the 1980s. In São Paulo the latter strategies were successful in winning a toe-hold in the state apparatus in the form of a Council on Women's Condition. The Council was only advisory, but it did supervise the implementation of family planning initiatives, and pushed through a special police precinct (staffed by women officers) to deal with cases of rape and violence against women. But even the Council was partisan insofar as it included representatives from the PMDB (the Party of the Brazilian Democratic Movement) but excluded all members of the PT (Workers' Party).

Just as social movements finally came to forge links with political parties (however reluctantly), they also made contact, formally and informally, with trade unions. Indeed unions and movements often had overlapping memberships, especially in the city; and many important movements emerged within the institutional contexts of state corporatism. This was the case of the teachers' movement in Mexico (Foweraker, 1993), and, to a significant degree, of the 'new unionism' within the ABC triangle of São Paulo [9] (Keck, 1989). Social movements in that city did not feel threatened by their relationship with the labour movement, and pursued their own policy in support of the striking workers. They were both motivated by the manifest failure of the state to manage the 'social question'. But unions too remained a predominantly male domain, and the women's movement made little headway in securing equal rights for women workers. Even where their legal rights made them equal, company practice and union compliance left them a long way short of real equality. In Argentina, women were confined to women's secretariats and committees within established unions, and their influence declined as their participation in manufacturing declined. In Chile women played little or no part in union leadership. Even in Brazil, where women mobilized massively both inside and outside the unions during the strikes of the late 1970s, the unions remained recalcitrant and failed to address the agenda of the women's movement.

The Influence of Social Movements on Political Parties

It is clear that 'contemporary social movements may well be charting new political terrain, but that domain is contiguous to and sometimes overlapped by the more traditional political terrain of trade unions, parties and the state' (Escobar and Alvarez, 1992:325). In Latin America it is also alleged that the rise of social movements 'challenges left political parties to develop more tolerant, democratic, and pluralistic political practices in spite of a weak democratic tradition' (Chinchilla, 1992:49); and the Latin American feminist movement continues to debate whether feminism should eschew traditional political parties or should take its struggle inside them (Sternbach et al., 1992). At the same time social movements have had a significant impact on political party formation and coalition, inspiring the Workers' Party (PT) in Brazil, the M–19/Democratic Alliance in Colombia and the Party of the Democratic Revolution (PRD) in Mexico. In Brazil, where political parties have always been notoriously unstable, the regions where contemporary social movements are strongest (São Paulo and Rio Grande do Sul) are also the regions with the best organized party systems. In general, the impact of social movements on political parties will often be felt most at municipal or regional rather than the national level.

The PT in Brazil grew directly out of the 'new unionism' in the ABC triangle of São Paulo, and the struggles of both unions and urban social movements against austerity policies (Sader, 1987b). It drew its leaders from the new union opposition, rural unions, and Catholic base communities (as well as from the Communist Party, the revolutionary left and the intelligentsia), and these leaders continued to be active in social movements. The Catholic base communities were especially important in linking neighbourhood associations to the labour movement and the PT, and the communities and movements have provided the party with popular content and support. The party, on the other hand, has helped organize collective action by women, blacks, ecologists and, of course, the unions within its 'own' trade union confederation, the CUT; and led the mobilization of many movements around the campaign for direct elections during the first months of 1984. (Indeed, the greater part of its organizational efforts during its early years was dedicated to opposing the military regime.) Thus, the PT can make plausible claims to be 'a party of a new type', [10] which drew together diverse popular sectors and the 'new union' movement, and succeeded in bringing social movements into the political arena (at least for a time). Under the military the party led a 'double existence' which combined the legal party with 'underground' militants who practised assembly-based direct democracy (Lowy, 1987); and this 'bottom up' style of organization influenced the national structure the party built in order to comply with the regime's conditions for legal recognition.

In authoritarian systems like the Brazilian one it is rare for a political party to represent social movements in the way the PT effectively did, although parties may build their programme and base their strategies on the political practices of these movements. The political line of the Communist Party in Franco's Spain was derived directly from the strategic discoveries of the opposition labour movement, the Workers' Commissions (Foweraker, 1989a). In other words, social movements help to shape the profile of political party opposition to the regime itself. In liberal democratic contexts, on the contrary, social movements have no constituency for changing the system overall, and are increasingly likely to build coalitions with parties and interest groups,[11] especially if these are prepared to respond to new issues by renewing their political agendas. In this way social movements are at most 'partial reform movements' which act as 'early warning systems' of pressures for change (Kaase, 1990).

Thus in Europe (and to a much lesser extent in North America) political parties have become adept at responding to social movements by preempting their issues and coopting their leaders. Social movements, on the other hand, may begin with an 'anti-institutional vocation' but they develop 'communication channels with traditional institutions' (Tarrow, 1990). Rather than promoting the realignment of established party systems, they are absorbed by them. In Latin America, on the contrary, political parties (with the exception of the PT and possibly the PRD) have had much less success in bringing social movements into the political arena, and have rather tended to displace them as soon as conditions are right (see Chapter 5). But the social movements have repeatedly called on the *state* to intervene in their favour, and so have been pulled willy-nilly into its sphere of influence and command. In both contexts these processes accelerate the institutionalization of the movements, and contribute to bring their 'cycles of protest' to a close. The result of this uneasy coalition with the old party system (Europe) or of this displacement by traditional political parties (Latin America) is the kind of 'composite and mottled effects' that add up to 'partial, disappointing and incremental reform' (Tarrow, 1990). But social movements cannot bring about change in a political vacuum and their impact 'will only be realized if there is some sort of institutional mediation, even at the cost of having dominant norms and values mould (or restrict) a large part of the movements' innovative potential' (Boschi, 1987b:23). In Latin America the question of the potential cost of such mediation is posed most acutely by the process of transition from authoritarian to democratic regimes, which is examined in the final chapter.

5 Social Movements and Democratic Transitions

Civil Society and Democratic Transitions

The most comprehensive theoretical account of modern social movements has asserted that the 'condition of possibility' of their emergence is 'the differentiated structure of modern civil society: legality, publicity, rights (to assemble, associate, and communicate free from external regulation), and the principles of democratic legitimacy' (Cohen and Arato, 1992:295).[1] But most modern social movements in Latin America arose under authoritarian regimes, and in far more constricted civil and political conditions (see Chapter 2). They do not therefore derive from democratic principles, but may contribute to create them through impelling political transitions from authoritarian to democratic regimes. There is no doubt that massive increases in social mobilization coincided with democratic transitions in countries like Brazil, Uruguay and Chile (Boschi, 1990), but the precise role of social movements in these transitions remains untheorized and unclear.

It has been suggested that harsh authoritarian regimes can easily quash social mobilization, but that the process of 'liberalization' can catalyse increasing opposition and a 'resurrection of civil society' (O'Donnell and Schmitter, 1986). But this is a vague assertion which differs little in its analytical purchase from Touraine's 'romantic moment ... when subjects come to an awareness ... of the distance that separates them from a hostile or meaningless order of things, in their desire for freedom and creation' (Touraine, 1988:160). In fact, even the recent contributions to the large literature on democratic transitions (e.g. Mainwaring, 1992) tend to eschew a more concrete analysis of social movements and their links with other political actors in the transition process (Levine, 1988). Hence social movements tend to be seen in uniform teleological terms as progressing inexorably from daily resistance to political protest to democratic project. This successfully avoids both the variety of democratic transitions[2] and the complexities of civil society. The result can only be banality: 'where popular leaders are committed to democracy and enjoy broad legitimacy in their organizations and movements, prospects for democracy are better' (Mainwaring, 1992:310).

One way forward is to broaden the focus. The literature on

social movements in Latin America has correctly emphasized their relation to the state. But the study of democratic transitions must focus first on the 'institutional make-up and internal articulation of civil society itself', before exploring the 'channels of influence between civil and political society and between both and the state' (Cohen and Arato, 1992:19). In other words the sociology (Chapter 3) and the politics (Chapter 4) of social movements must be combined, so that the defence of community and the formation of identity can be linked to the strategic choices and political projects which are capable of shaping political society. 'In a democratizing setting' the latter is the 'arena in which the polity specifically arranges itself for political contestation to gain control over public power and the state apparatus' (Stepan, 1988), and will therefore include constitutional provisions, electoral rules, political party programmes, party alliances and, finally, legislative procedure. But in what ways can civil society contribute to the constitution or reconstitution of this arena?

Social movements (it was argued in Chapter 3) are always rooted in social networks of family, community and face-to-face groups. Insofar as they articulate the 'felt needs' and proper demands of such networks they develop a kind of civic legitimacy, or 'recognized right to exist' (Cohen and Arato, 1992:48). This 'freedom of political identification' from being 'nullified or even determined solely by the authority of the national State' is something that 'democracy alone realizes' (Pizzorno, 1985:69), and civil society is the cradle of such collective identities. At the same time, these identities are not passive and indistinct parts of mass society but active and diverse groups which have specific political objectives and make specific demands about wages, houses, land, professional privileges, human rights, legal inequalities and fair elections. In short, they all contribute to the kind of civic and political 'associationalism' (Dahl, 1971; 1989) which is essential to political education and contestation. On the one hand they act as 'schools of democracy' (Foweraker, 1993) in the form of intellectual caucuses, popular assemblies, demonstrations, sit-ins and negotiations with political authorities. On the other they monitor government policies and initiatives and protest when rules are infringed or promises broken. In doing so they seek to restore the public sphere and reclaim this space from authoritarian constraints and control. Hence, the vindication of this public sphere is not pursued as a 'means to power' but as 'an end in itself', as a 'sphere of freedom' where political society can decide its own rules (Weffort, 1989).[3]

Social movements therefore have a role to play in reconstituting the conditions for the unimpeded operation of political society. The precise role will vary with the nature of the authoritarian regime. For example, it is argued that the Argentine military government atomized, depoliticized and privatized civil society while reducing and rigorously controlling the public sphere; whereas civil society seemed to survive authoritarian rule in Brazil with a proliferation of urban social movements, professional associations and popular church communities. Moreover (as suggested in Chapter 4) the state itself can often promote social movements, wittingly or unwittingly, with unpredictable political results. Civil society will therefore suffer different constraints and enjoy different degrees of freedom under different regimes and, consequently, social movement strategy will vary too. Just as negotiation with the state may be justified, despite the risks of cooptation, so may alliances with political parties, despite their expediency and their preoccupation with political power.

Yet all social movements under authoritarian regimes have one thing in common, and that is the discovery, vindication, defence and expansion of rights. It is therefore alleged that the political education and associationalism implicit in social movement activity generate new political demands that add up to a struggle for popular citizenship: social and economic demands meet the kind of political constraints which then generate an insistence on political rights (or on the political conditions for getting the original demands met) (Foweraker and Craig, 1990). Or social mobilization provokes the kind of political repression which obliges the movements to defend and expand their fundamental rights. But whatever the mechanism that translates petitions to demands and favours to rights, this is the essential step in the projection of social movements into political society.

There are potential problems with this interpretation. First, it is too naive and optimistic to assume 'an automatic and more or less direct path between the insistence on the right to running water, voting for the opposition and the demand for a change of political regime; and from the community movement, to the trade union movement, to the political party' (Caldeira, 1990:49). The involvement of urban movements from different regions of Brazil in municipal politics demonstrated that their main concerns were community needs and effective management, not political rights or political party programmes (Nunes and Jacobi, 1983). Secondly, social movements tend to pursue 'social rights' that are more strictly political entitlements than political rights, and that may therefore create not political citizens but political dependants or clients. In other words social movements aspire to citizenship in the Parsonian sense of equal conditions of participation in the societal community, rather than in the state. It then remains moot whether the struggle for social rights finally contributes directly or indirectly to the achievement of the core rights of political citizenship such as speech, belief, association, assembly and individual security, as well as substantive and procedural equality before the law.

This debate has a special resonance in Latin America where, historically, the cooptation of the labour movement into a clientelistic and corporative framework led to a political trade-off of the political rights of citizenship for the social rights of citizenship (for restricted and privileged sectors of the population) (Malloy, 1987). This inevitably undercut any sense of universal rights and promoted in their place a set of social benefits in the form of legal privileges and political prerogatives. There is no doubt that both sets of 'rights' (political and social) can be effective in mediating between civil society and the modern bureaucratic state (Cohen and Arato, 1992:441); but the struggle for social rights may be less effective in advancing the democratic agenda under patrimonial, clientelistic and authoritarian regimes. The key question then becomes whether the specific demands of social movements are satisfied through these particularistic power relations or transformed into more general demands for broader-based and political rights.

Social Movements and Political Society

In the liberal democratic context it is plausible to suggest that the trajectory of social movements is decisively shaped by the response of institutionalized forms of interest mediation, especially political parties (Scott, 1991). In the authoritarian context of Latin America it is similarly suggested that the impact of social movements on democratic transitions depends first and foremost on the form and timing of their insertion into the political process. In particular, 'new collective identities pushing for incorporation through social movements ... would have to be bound together by an effective party system' (Boschi, 1990:230). Social movements must therefore approach political society so that their goals are projected into the world of elections, party programmes and political bargaining. But this is not necessarily a simple continuation of the 'process of self organization of civil society', and it is often the continuing if restricted presence of political parties that is the 'natural focal point for negotiated transition' (Cohen and Arato, 1992:53). This means that parties and (the promise of) elections can themselves have 'remobilizing' consequences after a long period of political repression, and at an early moment in the transition process.

The role of social movements varies considerably from case to case. In Uruguay, military rule was largely restricted to the political realm, and economic life and the social structure continued undisturbed. But the military did move to repress and discipline the civil society, and this stimulated the emergence of social movements. The years between the plebiscite of 1980 and the transition of 1984 were a period of intense associationalism around specific interests but outside the framework of the state. There is little doubt that the series of alliances which constructed the National Concertation Project (CONAPRO) contributed to reconstitute political society and fill a temporary institutional void. This process was underpinned by the labour movement which both regained its traditional autonomy and strengthened its bargaining position through the merger of the Interunion Assembly of Workers (PIT) and the National Workers' Council (CNT). But political parties had continued strong and the party system had remained stable, and it was the parties that took control of the transition process. Social movements had played an important but limited and conjunctural role in creating the conditions for transition (and very few survived the transition itself).

Like Uruguay, Argentina was a predominantly urban society with a broad middle class. Unlike Uruguay, ungovernability had become normal, with an alternation of military and civilian regimes throughout its modern history, and especially after 1955. The working class was highly organized within the Peronist (Justicialist) Party, but had never been incorporated into the political system. Indeed, the political party system itself had never been successfully institutionalized, so that strong social forces tended to clash violently in the absence of stable forms of political mediation. Since political parties themselves continued strong, the result was 'strong subcultures and a weak system' (Boschi, 1990) characterized by 'anarchic corporatism' (O'Donnell, 1984:24). Although successive military interventions reflected continuing attempts to prevent the Peronists taking over government, they finally damaged the legitimacy of any elected government and reduced civil commitment to democratic politics. Civil society was therefore strong, at least in its 'corporatist' forms, but political society was weak, and social movements could therefore achieve little political purchase within the transition process. Their importance under military rule was restricted to changes in civil society for the most part, and social mobilization fell far short of precipitating democratic transition.

In Chile, the party system and its links with popular sectors and social movements had always been central to the political system overall. The suppression of political parties therefore posed acute strategic problems for the opposition to the military dictatorship: some new movements arose within civil society, under the aegis of the Catholic Church, for example, but party activists continued to play a key role in their organization and, although parties tended to react to government initiatives rather than take their own (at least before 1983) they nonetheless stimulated most forms of social mobilization. The huge mobilization of May 1983, initiated by the Copper Workers' Union's call for a day of national protest, was successful in uniting middle and popular sectors for the first time in many years. But the strength of the repression, and selective cooptation of middle-class demands, left subsequent mobilization to the more radical student and youth groups, especially on the urban periphery. Protests continued throughout 1983 and 1984, but (as noted towards the end of Chapter 4) political party divisions within the opposition now made mobilization increasingly difficult. Indeed, the main problem for the opposition from the middle 1980s was 'how to overcome the fragmentation produced by divisions among the parties' (Garretón, 1989a:173).

Social movements in Chile did not therefore fill a void left by political parties. The parties remained intact and remarkably unchanged. Possibly for this reason they tended to lose touch with social mobilizations at critical moments, until the opposition to the dictatorship was split between the party opposition and the 'social' opposition of popular sector organizations of the urban poor, students and workers. These organizations were plagued with problems of daily survival, while the parties remained wedded to their traditional political ways and could not easily reform their relations with the social movements. Since popular leaders tended to take a 'maximalist' stance which sought confrontation, the division between political parties and their social base looked likely to grow deeper. This division could be said to reflect a split between the 'instrumental' politics of the party leaders and the 'expressive' politics of young urban and student activists (see Chapter 3).

Although all parties in Chile backed mobilization, they set different goals. The Christian Democrats and the 'centre' sought negotiation; the left parties wanted to bring down the regime. The Assembly of Civility (*Asemblea de la Civilidad*) of 1986 aimed to overcome these divisions by bringing together professional associations, labour unions and, in principle, the popular urban sectors, as well as women's organizations and human rights groups. But, despite the Assembly's massive mobilization of July 1986, both the opposition in general and the labour unions in particular remained divided; while political party rivalries undermined the first Unitary Congress of Urban Settlers. The student and women's movements escaped the worst of the factionalism for a time, but finally came to feel its adverse effects. In these conditions social movements were most concerned to preserve their identity and forge effective leadership, while both parties and movements remained preoccupied with short-term survival tactics and fleeting political alliances. The movements' engagement with political society did little to develop a coherent strategy of democratic transition until the arrival of the 'constitutional moment' of the plebiscite.

The diversity and complexity of these different cases invalidate the simple, dichotomous scheme that separates the democratic struggles of the advanced capitalist countries from the popular struggles of the so-called Third World. According to Laclau and Mouffe, the diversity of social antagonisms in 'central' countries encourages the multiplication of democratic struggles but prevents them from constituting a 'people'. 'On the contrary, in the countries of the Third World, imperialist exploitation and the predominance of brutal and centralized forms of domination tend from the beginning to endow the popular struggle with a centre, with a single and clearly defined enemy' (Laclau and Mouffe, 1985:131). In Latin America, therefore, the diversity of democratic struggles is reduced to a single antagonism between the 'principle of domination' vested in the state and the people (Laclau, 1977). In short, this is not democratic struggle at all, but popular struggle where 'discourses tendentially construct the division of a single social space into two opposing fields' (Laclau and Mouffe, 1985:131).

The clear implication here is that all social movements, by the very fact of insisting on their autonomy from the authoritarian state, automatically become part of a political movement which is formed as a broad coalition around an uncomplicated oppositional identity (Munck, n.d.). Moreover, since 'political space' is increasingly divided between the 'state' and the 'people', all strategic calculations and disputes are subsumed within the single goal of bringing down the authoritarian regime. But nothing in this approach captures the real process of identity formation, the real motives of social mobilization, or the real complexities of strategic calculation, especially with regard to political party alliances. In short, it represents a massive oversimplification of the realities of popular struggle in Latin America. Laclau and Mouffe go on to argue that in a modern or 'hegemonic form of politics', e.g. in Europe, the frontiers between antagonistic social forces are inherently unstable and porous. But they fail to note that under the authoritarian regimes of Latin America the frontiers between civil society and the state are equally unstable, 'negotiated' and subject to the outcomes of strategic advance and retreat. They also ignore the political and cultural differences which character-

ize the legal and institutional terrains that conjoin state and civil
society in different countries of the continent.

Social Movements, Rights and Citizenship

Social movements in Latin America struggle to get their demands
met, and increasingly these demands have been stated in terms of
rights (Cardoso, 1983). Where authoritarian regimes compressed
the public sphere, social movements asserted their right to expand
it. 'The suppression of some traditional rights produced a redefinition and expansion of the understanding of rights ... to reconquer
rights which traditionally existed and to fight for new rights' (Mainwaring and Viola, 1984:33). Where state policies excluded the
popular sectors and denied them a voice, social movements
mounted 'a struggle for equal rights, justice ... and the recognition
of a minimum threshold of rights associated with belonging to and
inclusion in the social system' (Jelin, 1990:206). The struggle for
rights demonstrates that 'while the state is the agency of the
legalization of rights, it is neither their source nor the basis of their
validity. Rights begin as claims asserted by groups and individuals
in the public spaces of an emerging civil society' (Cohen and Arato,
1992:446) and, in this sense, political rights are positive rights of
equal participation rather than 'freedoms' or 'liberties'.

The assertion of the political right to participate is an
assertion of citizenship: these 'struggles from below, in which
subordinate social sectors redefine their identities and their
rights' are 'an attempt to widen their space for action and
extend the boundaries of their social and political citizenship'
(Jelin, 1990:5). In small, popular, church communities 'individuals are being citizens and are also exercising a right which they
cannot take for granted, namely that of assembly' (Lehmann,
1990b:153). In entering the public sphere for the first time
women are demanding recognition of their rights as citizens
(and rejecting representation by men, whether as spouses,
neighbourhood leaders or politicians) (Safa, 1990). In the countryside rural cooperatives 'bolster citizenship ... by creating
rights and an awareness of rights among members', and even
struggles over land are mainly 'founded on an objection to
violations of rights' (Lehmann, 1990b:163). In the majority,
demands for rights are demands for fair dealing by the authorities, and this is what spurs social movements to 'oppose
corruption and favour transparency ... oppose arbitrariness and
favour due process' (Lehmann, 1990b:151). The result has been
to place 'the theme of citizenship – that is, of the human and
civil rights of persons – at the forefront of popular movements,

avoiding the assumption of earlier radicalisms that there could be no citizenship without a total transformation of society' (Lehmann, 1990b:147). Citizenship, in short, must be achieved in the here and now: 'Now we demand what we deserve, what corresponds to us as citizens of this country. We demand what is legally ours. We demand our rights.'[4]

The struggle for rights has more than a merely rhetorical impact. The insistence on the rights of free speech and assembly is a precondition of the kind of collective (and democratic) decision-making which educates citizens. The 'affirmation of the right to specificity and difference' by women or ethnic groups (Jelin, 1990:206) is a precondition of plural and democratic society (Pizzorno, 1985). In other words, 'the practice of rights and the corresponding forms of social learning help ... to establish a political culture that values societal self-organization' (Cohen and Arato, 1992:440). But social movements also press to put rights (labour rights, land rights, human rights) on the active political agenda, and the denial or abuse of these rights then produces 'political antagonism' (Mouffe, 1988). The exercise of rights challenges the political order and, in authoritarian conditions, even 'expressive' collective action can amount to a claim on citizenship. Social movements seek to enter the political stage and also to rewrite the political script (Jelin, 1990:5).[5]

However, social movements in Latin America often press 'economic corporate' demands before all others. Whether these economic and social demands later take on a political thrust or not, the movements take 'rights of citizenship' to include 'as much social rights (in the specific case of collective consumption) as political rights' (Nunes and Jacobi, 1983:56). Thus the struggle of urban social movements to defend the land and the communal space which will allow them a home is a struggle for 'urban citizenship' (Massolo and Ronner, 1983); and the savagery of much urban speculation and exploitation makes of the Latin American city 'a city without citizens' (Castells, 1983:175). In general, it is inescapable that many movements are based on primary groups 'rather than the secondary, professional and more anonymous groupings which embody a liberal image of active citizenship' (Lehmann, 1990b:154), and are therefore more easily subject to clientelistic control and paternalistic manipulation. Moreover, it is argued that 'social rights of the entitlement type achieve the benefits of membership for individuals as clients rather than as citizens' (Cohen and Arato, 1992:446), and that the notion of social rights 'actually contradicts the notion of citizenship, which cannot be made consistent with any form of paternalism' (Cohen and Arato, 1992:127). But if there are doubts regarding the contribution of social rights to citizenship, they apply more to the highly bureaucratized welfare apparatuses of European states than to the precarious provision of social benefits in Latin America. The real doubt is 'whether benefits whose exercise does not depend primarily on the free activity of the beneficiaries are rights at all' (Cohen and Arato, 1992:446), and there is no doubt that social rights in Latin America are only won intermittently through recurrent mobilization.

Yet social rights may play a different role in closely controlled corporatist institutions and in the highly clientelistic and corporatized systems of countries like Mexico and Brazil. (The political cultures of Chile and Uruguay were both less 'corporatized' and somewhat more sensitive to the universal rights of citizenship.) In particular, it was argued above that organized labour's 'quest for particular privileges undercut universal notions of citizenship crucial to modern democratic systems' (Malloy, 1987:254), and since labour leaders secured as much or more access to social benefits under authoritarian as under democratic regimes they did not develop a primary commitment to democracy either in principle or for its social welfarism. But the extension of benefits came at the expense of rights, and the labour movements of the 1970s and 1980s put labour rights back onto the political agenda, while the corporatist cooptation of labour created an institutional context that favoured the growth of these movements (Foweraker, 1989a) (see Chapter 4). In Mexico, powerful movements within state-chartered corporations shook the foundations of the political system (Foweraker, 1993). In Brazil, the 'new unionism' of the late 1970s insisted that the workers themselves should decide their own forms of organization,[6] while the chaotic strikes of 1979 seemed inspired by 'an assertion of rights rather than a demand for concessions' (Keck, 1989:289). Direct bargaining between employers and 'authentic' labour leaders bypassed the corporatist controls of the state, so securing the de facto right to strike and challenging the core of the exclusionary labour system. State repression only accelerated the collapse of legal constraints, so freeing labour for fuller citizenship: how could workers be citizens of the nation when they were less (or more) than citizens in labour relations (Keck, 1989)?

Mobilization and Negotiation

Social movements have to mobilize to press their demands and vindicate their rights. This mobilization can appear cyclical, and the movements themselves discontinuous. Immediate demands can be satisfied. The costs of mobilization are high. Alliances are hard to achieve. But the discontinuity may be more apparent than real, with new movements emerging from old ones, and old movements building a collective memory of victories and defeats. Moreover, the social needs that drive the movements are not temporary, and the rights they claim are not conjunctural. In Brazil the wide range of new movements which emerged in the late 1970s focused on everything from the cost of living to gender and race issues, and mobilized poor neighbourhoods, squatter settlements and working-class communities. The new urban middle class was also important in this 'associational impulse' (Boschi, 1987b), and the middle-class and the popular sectors achieved a temporary alliance during the campaign for direct elections (*diretas, já*) in 1984; but the alliance was precariously constructed around the one single demand, and dissolved immediately the congressional vote was lost on 25 April. The campaign clearly expressed a popular search for a lasting democratic solution; but it also revealed the volatility of popular protest and the difficulty of sustaining high degrees of mobilization. Similarly in Chile, middle-class and popular sectors mobilized together during 1983, but the different groups lacked any principle of unity beyond 'Democracy Now', and so did not conceive a 'set of intermediate goals that could maintain a high level of mobilization and force negotiation with the regime' (Garretón, 1989a:153). Hence the mobilization subsided and returned to recurrent agitation by the most militant groups, with the struggle for democracy condemned to 'mobilization without political strategy'. An analogous story could be told of Cárdenas' campaign for the presidency of Mexico, and the massive mobilization inspired by the Democratic National Front before and after the elections of July 1988 (Foweraker, 1993: ch. 11). The political capital generated by this upsurge of popular energy then dissipated in the absence of a negotiating strategy (or was squandered by the refusal to negotiate with the incumbent regime).

Social movements mobilize to press their demands, but mobilization necessarily entails negotiation with state agencies and political authorities if these demands are to be won. Hence it cannot be correct to impute a vague progressive content to popular collective action. Social movements are not 'radical democrats' yearning for an egalitarian democracy (Mainwaring and Viola, 1984:23). They insist on autonomy not as an absolute value but as a precondition of effective negotiation (see Chapter 4), and winning the right to negotiate may imply more pluralism but does not automatically advance a process of democratic transition. Urban social movements in Brazil mobilized 'originally in confrontation with the state in the attempt to open space for underrepresented interests, or to assure entrance of new groups into the political arena' (Boschi, 1987a:184).

New councils were set up to channel their demands, and these certainly appeared more accessible than the old clientelistic networks; but it is difficult to decide whether this was participation in decision-making or a new form of cooptation. In any event, the longer-term activity of most social movements involves 'permanent negotiation', and the very fact of putting and negotiating demands may disseminate the sense of rights and the idea of citizenship. The transitions to democracy themselves tend to occur through a complicated process of negotiation, but social movements rarely have direct access to it (Assies et al., 1991).

Once negotiation is routinized, the state looks less like an enemy of the social movements. In Brazil, at least, the centralizing and 'developmentalist' state carried through administrative reforms and improved the reach and delivery of public services. Since the military governments continued to compete for the popular vote they kept negotiations open and sometimes made concessions. The Figueiredo government (1979–85) began to expand popular housing projects, and implemented a wage policy that actually favoured the poorest of the workers (before the crisis of 1982 put a stop to these popular policies). In themselves these changes cannot demonstrate a greater commitment to popular participation, let alone democracy. They may simply indicate the growing ability of the state to absorb popular demands (Cardoso, 1983; Scherer-Warren and Krische, 1987). But the relationship between state and social movements is certainly more complex than simple confrontation.

Nonetheless there are still severe limits to what social movements can achieve through this combination of mobilization and negotiation. First, there are the enduring problems created by populism and clientelism. On the one hand, the apparatuses of the authoritarian state continued to use these well-tried mechanisms of cooptation and control. Despite the multiplication of autonomous urban social movements in Mexico in the late 1970s and early 1980s, and the national alliance strategy of the CONAMUP (National Coordinating Committee of Urban Popular Movements), the majority of popular organizations in the city continued to be managed and manipulated by the CNOP (National Confederation of Popular Organizations), one of the three main state-chartered union corporations run by the ruling party, the PRI (Institutional Revolutionary Party). On the other, the same mechanisms are reproduced through the projection of social movements into political society and their initial imbrication with political parties. Social movements fielded candidates in the more urban areas of Brazil for the 1982 elections, but the clientelistic ties to party machines either divided and demobilized the movements or led to the creation of parallel and more conservative popular organizations.

Secondly, the strategy of mobilization and negotiation can only be successful where government itself (or the public administration) is prepared to negotiate. Despite the almost monthly demonstrations launched by popular organizations in Chile during the wave of protest of 1983 the military government survived the crisis and proceeded 'according to the institutional design and timetable set forth in the constitution' (Garretón, 1989a:154). Although the government made specious concessions the 'so-called political opening did not involve establishing an arena for representation but only tolerating an informal and reversible political space' (Garretón, 1989a:157). Moreover, as confrontation replaced negotiation it raised the profile of the most radical and violent protesters (students and urban youth) and isolated them from other popular sectors, so making mass-based mobilization more difficult. The initial involvement of middle-class sectors in the protests, and the place of the most powerful union confederation (the CTC) in the vanguard, had reduced popular fears of a massacre and slowed the government's repressive response. But ultimately thousands of troops were deployed on the streets of Santiago, and hundreds and finally thousands of protesters were detained, tortured, exiled or disappeared. In Argentina, on the other hand, the military government did not even wait for popular protest before moving to evict hundreds of thousands of squatters (*villeros*) from the shanty towns of Buenos Aires; and neighbourhood councils could do nothing to prevent the continual violence except file judicial complaints (Silva and Schuurman, 1989). When an upsurge of social mobilization in these urban districts was finally provoked by the punitive tax hikes of 1982, the government again refused to negotiate. In neither case did popular protest by social movements succeed in shaking the confidence of the military regime.

Even in the 'limiting case' of Argentina, however, it has been argued that social movements did play a role in democratizing political culture (Mainwaring and Viola, 1984), developing community and self-government (Jelin, 1987), and revitalizing local politics. In short, it is recognized that social movements do have a role 'in the creation of at least the foundations of new democratic cultures' (Boschi, 1987a:185). But most commentators are sceptical of the impact of social movements on democratic transition (Assies et al., 1991), and instead emphasize the salience of elite actors and political pacts in this process (Higley and Gunther, 1992). Social movements may practice democracy (in some degree at some times), and social mobilization may encourage more democratic social relations, but it remains difficult and often impossible to institutionalize these effects, or to achieve institutional guarantees for popular participation (Assies et al., 1991). As observed on several occasions, social movements tend to express specific and transitory demands, and their objectives change, either because of internal disputes and factionalism or because of state initiatives. Hence, widespread mobilization by social movements may find little institutional response and 'scholars should acknowledge just how limited their short-term impact really is' (Boschi, 1987a:184).

There are reasons to take issue with this position. First, the analysts tend to have a very formal view of the linkages between social movements and political institutions. They ignore the longer-term impact of mobilization and demand-making on the broad contours of the legal-institutional terrain linking civil society to the state (see Chapter 4); and close empirical study can demonstrate in some detail the success of social movements in reconfiguring this terrain (Foweraker, 1989a; 1993; Foweraker and Craig, 1990). In short, social movements are capable of disputing state policies and catalysing institutional reforms (Scherer-Warren and Krische, 1987). Secondly, the analysts are too pessimistic regarding the projection of social movements into political society. For democratic transition to occur there must be the 'differentiation of a political element capable of strategic consideration' (Cohen and Arato, 1992:470), and the partial cooptation or 'institutionalization' of social movements may be a proper price to pay for the emergence of agile political actors that can negotiate with incumbent regimes. The Chilean process finally came close to this model, and the Mexican process may yet get there. Thirdly, even if it is agreed that 'the governing bloc must decompose' before the transition can come about (Garretón, 1989a:262), social movements may still be important in widening the breach: 'without some initial cracks in the authoritarian coalitions their impact was limited, but once such cracks appeared they bolstered the efforts to oust autocratic governments' (Mainwaring, 1992). There is no doubt that the direct elections campaign of 1984 in Brazil succeeded in bringing the transition forward if not actually in bringing it about. Finally, it may be prudent to reject the characterization of democratic transition as a 'one-off' historical event: social movements have only recently begun to insist on the rights of citizenship, and democratic transitions themselves may have some way to go.

Democratic Transition and the Decline of Social Movements

At the moment of regime crisis social mobilization can make a difference to the fact and the outcome of democratic transition. The impetus of mobilization can open or widen breaches in the dominant coalition, as well as influencing the strategic calculations of elite actors in the economy and the state (Foweraker, 1989a). If the crisis continues, repression becomes more difficult, and social movements may perceive new opportunities for winning their political demands. For a time mobilization becomes more important than sustained organization, but the movements begin to lose impetus once negotiations begin with the incumbent regime, and parties or proto-parties begin to move to centre stage. Broad alliances between movements become less likely with the shift from 'economic corporate' to party political and electoral objectives. On the model of 'transition through transaction' (Share and Mainwaring, 1986), authoritarian elites manage to retain inside influence over the state apparatuses, and the process of compromise and pacts leads to strong institutional continuities. Administrative cadres are often unchanged and the executive remains predominant over a weak and unstable party system. Since social movements were unsuccessful in institutionalizing the degrees of representation achieved through mobilization and negotiation they are now sidelined from policy-making and removed from the centres of power. Their uncertain connection with political parties means that they have no realistic hope of defining the political agenda (while the parties lack insertion in social movement 'constituencies'). In short, with the transition to a democratic set of rules, social movements enter into decline.

Since the recent democratic transitions in Latin America took place in conditions of economic crisis, social movements mainly failed to influence the distribution of real resources in their favour, and so lost some of their *raison d'être*. This effect was reinforced by the austerity programmes espoused by the International Monetary Fund and the foreign banks, while neo-liberal economic reforms in general responded to a conception of civil society as a market economy of atomized individuals, and not a social arena for collective political action (Munck, n.d.). The lack of any effective link with political parties meant that the movements were drawn into the sphere of the state, where they were again subject to populist manoeuvres and clientelist tactics (Mainwaring, 1987). In Brazil, especially, the movements' attempts to secure corporative protection in the new constitution led to new forms of corporatist control. Political elites jockeyed for position, the executive tried to buy support in congress, politicians tried to buy a new electorate, and all this catalysed clientelism and promoted the come-back of populist politicians. Moreover, since parties were poorly entrenched and unattached to large constituencies, they could not act as brokers in distributional conflicts, and so the problem of corruption could spread unimpeded.

Above all, with the transition to democracy, the struggle for citizenship moves to the constitutional sphere, and social movements lose their pre-eminent role as defenders and promoters of legal and political rights. Every state administration which is organized through bureaucratic power relations will seek to institutionalize positive law and so create 'subjects capable of political obligation, and later the rights of citizens' (Cohen and Arato, 1992:439), and a newly democratic regime will seek to build its legitimacy by insisting on these rights. In other words, citizenship becomes an identity that is defended and disseminated by the state against all class and regional differences, and against the specific identities and claims of social movements (Touraine, 1988:75). But social movements had often pressed for citizenship rights, and had challenged social and political institutions to see these rights enshrined in law and put into practice. Insofar as this occurs through democratic transition, many of their demands are met, and their political energy begins to dissipate. 'Successful social movements inevitably lose their reason for being' (Jaquette, 1989:194).

Social Movements and Political Society Revisited

Under authoritarian regimes civil society itself had become politicized, partly because of the total or partial suppression of the main actors of political society. With the advent of democracy, civil and political societies are more clearly differentiated (Munck, n.d.), and social movements must learn new rules of the political game. But it is suggested that the movements 'emerged in an authoritarian situation which continues to define their approach to politics' (Mainwaring and Viola, 1984:44), and that they are unable to adapt 'the confrontational tactics of the transition period to the strategies of negotiation and compromise necessitated by the new democratic status quo' (Escobar and Alvarez, 1992). In short, 'these movements and these protagonists have not learnt how to deal with a democratic scenario and have little historical memory of how to do so' (Jelin, 1990:108).

These observations recall Laclau and Mouffe's assertion that democratic struggle is inevitably more diverse, decentred and 'multipositional' than a common popular struggle against an authoritarian regime (Laclau and Mouffe, 1985), and there is little doubt that during democratic transition the number of social movements multiplies, as does the diversity of direct channels to the state apparatus (Cardoso, 1987). But different parts of the state apparatus can be either receptive or repressive, and social movements can insist on their autonomy or accept clientelism, depending on the circumstances. The relationship with the state remains ambiguous, and the process of political representation is tortuous, unpredictable and reversible. For the social movements post-transition political society becomes what the Brazilians call a *jôgo surdo*, a 'dance of the deaf'. The rules may be new but they are not clear (and they vary according to local and regional context). Most popular leaders would therefore need no convincing that 'the process of establishing a democracy is a process of institutionalizing uncertainty' (Przeworski, 1986:58).

The difficulties that social movements may encounter in political society are compounded by political parties. There is no 'natural' affinity between the local, regional or 'corporate' demands of social movements and the national programmes of political parties (Tamayo, 1987; Nunes and Jacobi, 1983) (see Chapter 4). While parties seek to secure power through forms of territorial representation, social movements continue to press for material benefits and 'substantive' democracy through direct participation.[7] Local leaders may well view party militants with suspicion (Schneider, 1992) and seek to bypass the parties by a direct approach to municipal authorities and government agencies. Parties, on the other hand, may try to attract local leaders, but soon discover that it is not easy to take the local out of the leader (Cardoso, 1987). It can be argued that in an ideal world social movements should move beyond their local context and promote 'the formation of a civic culture' (Boschi, 1987a:202), but their successful insertion into the Workers' Party (PT) in Brazil retarded the party's elaboration of a national and popular programme.

As democratic transition proceeds, political parties re-emerge and begin to compete for popular support among social movements, not least because their bargaining power depends on this support in some degree (Mainwaring, 1992). At the same time, some social movement activists will seek political party affiliation to advance their own careers (Cardoso, 1987). Social movements cannot therefore escape the increasing salience of partisan politics in a more open political society (Mainwaring, 1987) and 'the democratization process they help encourage creates the conditions for internal division and competition' (Mainwaring and Viola, 1984:44). As a result, conflicts arise both within the movements and between movements and political parties; and movements and parties draw further apart and closer together in a fluctuating rhythm (Cardoso, 1987). In Argentina the democratic transition, and a larger margin of legal manoeuvre, accentuated the divisions between different urban social movements (Silva and Schuurman, 1989). In Bolivia the advent of democratic government in October 1982 seemed to catalyse factional strife within the rural movements (Jelin, 1990). In Brazil the New Republic reinforced the heterogeniety of the social movements and left them increasingly isolated.

The democratic transitions of Latin America have depended on covert and exclusionary pacts (Cohen and Arato, 1992; Higley and Gunther, 1992) between parties which are 'elitist, hierarchical and socially conservative' (Jaquette, 1990:206). Their most likely outcome is therefore a 'restricted democracy' where social movements are 'isolated, repressed or marginalized' (Mainwaring and Viola, 1984:46). But the real result varies according to the political culture. The strong state apparatuses and highly developed party systems of Chile and Uruguay appeared to displace social movements and leave them diminished (Cohen and Arato, 1992; Escobar and Alvarez, 1992). In both countries the party system remained intact and re-emerged first to assert political identification (a reflection of political memory), and then to channel political representation (Boschi, 1990). Social movements sought institutional expression in parties, unions and NGOs, and could not easily contest the broad consensus that supported the traditional democratic way of life. In Argentina, on the other hand, although social movements like the human rights movement managed to influence party platforms for the 1983 elections, they did not succeed in securing more permanent forms of representation, and the human rights groups in particular rapidly lost ground in succeeding years. Thus the movements in Argentina tended to suffer not from democratic but from 'deeply entrenched authoritarian traditions' (Mainwaring and Viola, 1984:43).[8] In Brazil social movements found a real voice in the authentically new Workers' Party, and they mobilized to give the party a mass character (Lowy, 1987). Rather than re-emerging from authoritarian rule, the Workers' Party emerged anew as a response to popular struggle under authoritarian rule, and may yet serve as the centrepiece of an electoral coalition that controls national government.

During democratic transitions political parties have done what was necessary to prevent authoritarian reversals. The very fact of elections implies negotiations between opposition parties and the incumbent regime, often leading to a more than representative share of the vote for parties close to the regime. To obtain such a result, social movements have to be controlled and demobilized (Cohen and Arato, 1992). In Brazil the presence of the Workers' Party encouraged many movements to participate in the elections of 1982 and in the campaign for direct presidential elections of 1984. But regional opposition victories in 1982 and the diversions of the national campaign of 1984 both tended to demobilize the movements as vehicles for community or sectoral demands (Boschi, 1987b). Even in Brazil, therefore, social movements risked demobilization if they participated in party politics (Scherer-Warren and Krische, 1987). In Chile the more moderate movements were rapidly drawn into political society as soon as a date had been set for the constitutional plebis-cite, and grassroots mobilization only lasted as long as the plebiscitary and electoral campaigns themselves. Participation rates dropped dramatically after March 1990, indicating that social movements were likely to be demobilized permanently by the return to democratic politics.

Despite this recent evidence the historical record has tended to show that electoral politics legitimates other forms of associa-tion and protest by providing legal protections. The rights to organize, recruit, speak, assemble, publicize and demonstrate are essential to multiparty systems with universal suffrage, and it is difficult for governments to withhold these rights from other social actors, even in 'elite' or 'restricted' democracies. In this way 'state toleration or promotion of various sorts of electoral associa-tion ... provided a warrant and a model for the action of associa-tions that were quasi-electoral, semielectoral or even nonelectoral' (Tilly, 1984:311). In Latin America too it is not impossible that the entrenchment of electoral politics will finally favour the spread of social movements (and the character of social movements might change as a result) (Escobar and Alvarez, 1992). There is little doubt that, even in the southern cone, democratic tran-sitions have already helped to rebuild the labour movement (Tour-aine, 1987). Outside the southern cone, social movements have challenged the political parties' monopoly of representation in two of the continent's more resilient democracies, Colombia and Venezuela (Escobar and Alvarez, 1992). The different regional movements grouped within the Democratic Alliance M-19 in Colombia fleetingly gained a national profile in the general elec-tions of May 1990, in their continuing attempt to fill the void left by the violence and corruption of the two major parties, and in both Colombia and Venezuela social movements have sought to deepen and expand the democratic arrangements forged through the elite pacts of the 1950s. It is not inconceivable that they may play a similar role in Brazil or the southern cone countries in years to come.

Democratic Transitions and the Women's Movement

The military and authoritarian regimes of Latin America had a specific impact on women. First, they were relegated to the private sphere. Despite their increasing participation in the labour market and their educational attainments, they were confined to the home; and the governments of Chile and Argentina maintained the *potestad marital* which gave men full control over the person and property of their spouses. In the public sphere, laws, employment programmes, jobs and pay scales all prejudiced women, and women played almost no part in government itself (Valenzuela, 1990). Secondly, their families were then assaulted by intimidation, torture and disappearances; women themselves were subjected to sexual torture, and family ties were manipulated to increase the effectiveness of torture (Jaquette, 1989). Thirdly, economic crisis and austerity policies threatened the survival of poor families on the urban periphery and so mobilized women to defend their livelihoods. In short, by reinforcing the authoritarian culture of the family, fusing the questions of women's rights and human rights, and raising the stakes of economic survival, the military governments effectively politicized the private sphere, mobilized women for social action, and stimulated them to join the civilian opposition. Hence, the women's movements were 'shaped from the beginning by their role in opposition to the military dictatorships. Ironically, military authoritarian rule, which intentionally depoliticized men and restricted the rights of "citizens", had the unintended consequence of mobilizing marginal and normally apolitical women' (Jaquette, 1989:5).

The conditions of military rule catalysed three main kinds of women's organization (Jaquette, 1989). Initially the most visible were the human rights groups which protested the detentions, the torture and the disappearances. At the core of organizations like the Permanent Assembly for Human Rights and the Families of the Detained and Disappeared (in Argentina) were the relatives of those who had suffered at the hands of the regimes. In some cases their activism grew out of their work in the popular church and therefore received some support from the church (but not in Argentina). Less visible were the properly feminist groups which recruited middle-class professionals and women on the left who were frustrated by the failure of left-wing parties to take women's issues seriously. Their numbers and their ideas multiplied with the return of exiles from Europe and North America, and they began to provide legal aid, counselling and education to torture victims, women's groups and the broader opposition. Finally, there were the associations of poor urban women who were forced to respond to the removal of state benefits and subsidies, and to the lack of basic services. They set up communal kitchens, infant feeding centres and neighbourhood workshops, and attracted support from international agencies and the church. It was the question of economic survival that shaped the social agenda of the women's movement and, crucially, gave it a mass base.

Take the case of Chile. Despite its policies the regime sought the support of women, whom it considered to be dedicated to the superior values of abnegation and service, and therefore its 'natural' allies (Valenzuela, 1990). The government set up grand women's organizations along military lines, while the National Secretariat for Women attempted to build civil allegiance. However, the objective was not to improve the conditions of poor women but to make them resigned to their lot. But poverty and dereliction encouraged a different kind of participation. The church fostered community struggles, the left organized neighbourhood associations, and the existing network of 'mothers' centres' (CEMAs) were turned to the opposition's own purposes. The result was an explosion of female organizations, with more than a thousand Popular Economic Organizations in Greater Santiago by 1985. During the 1970s women had staffed various human rights groups and carried out solidarity work with prisoners and their families, and in 1979 a women's committee of the Chilean Human Rights Commission was formed. By the early 1980s women were active in three major female confederations. But the great strength of the women's groups was their capacity to act in unity and to mobilize independently of the political parties (Garretón, 1989a), witnessed in the massive demonstration of Women for Life in December 1983. This mobilizational capacity gave women a high profile during the democratic transition. At the moment of the plebiscite a Women's Command coordinated the attempts of party activists to reach women voters and, for the first time, the campaign projected women's issues into the struggles of political society. Despite the traditionally conservative pattern of female voting in Chile, 52 per cent of women voted against the prolongation of the Pinochet dictatorship.

Chile was not the only country where the women's movement had a mass political base. In Brazil the church urged women to join community struggles, left-wing parties placed female militants on the urban periphery, and the military itself allowed women the leeway to organize (while repressing other sectors) because it did not view women as 'political' (Alvarez, 1989). As the regime 'liberalized', the movement grew rapidly. In Argentina, on the other hand, the church gave tacit support to the military, the left was decimated in the Dirty War (the name given to the military regime's assault on civil society), and women's militancy was reduced to and concentrated in the human rights organizations (so explaining both their high profile and their isolation). But even in Argentina housewives' movements spread across the urban periphery during the latter months of 1982 (the so-called *vecinazos*) and, at the time of the transition, 'each of the parties rushed to constitute its own women's front' (Feijoó, 1989:81) in order to win the women's vote. Alfonsín's Radical Civic Union took the Madres' slogan, 'We are life', as the leitmotif of its own campaign, and its success was owing to the women's overwhelming support.

For all these reasons it is legitimate to take the women's movement as a litmus test for the fate of social movements following democratic transitions (Safa, 1990). In Argentina the women's movement faced the challenge of moving from the grassroots of civil society into political society, and of maintaining its impetus without becoming just another political lobby. The most salient of the human rights groups, the Mothers of the Plaza de Mayo, were disappointed by the government's decision not to pursue those responsible for the Dirty War, and subsequently had difficulty in adapting to democratic politics. The government did create a National Women's Agency within the Ministry of Social Security, but many within the movement saw this as a palliative measure designed to demobilize them. It is true that the Argentine version of *potestad marital* was modified, divorce was legalized, child care facilities were extended, contraception was made available, and domestic violence against women was widely debated. But party leaders did not fulfil their campaign promises, and women's political careers were largely confined to government programmes like the National Food Programme and the National Literacy Campaign.

In Brazil a National Council on Women's Rights was established following the transition of 1985, but very few women were elected to parliaments at state or federal levels, women's demands found only a faint reflection in the Constitution, and the women's movement declined. In a typical trajectory for social movements, the movement was removed from decision-making arenas where (male dominated) party and interest group politics took over; and as women's groups also changed tack to pressure group politics they increasingly courted cooptation and division (Alvarez, 1990). The only other mass-based movement in Chile also ran increased risks of cooptation, but this time by political parties rather than the state apparatus itself. The male dominated parties set up women's sections which were mere appendices of the power structure, and so the principled adhesion to sexual equality was never put into practice. The parties had begun by addressing gender concerns, but switched to support of the family as their central social policy. Very few women were elected in the first elections of the transition, and so had no significant place in either legislature or executive (Chuchryk, 1989). It is therefore not surprising that in Uruguay, where the movement had nothing like the impetus achieved in Chile and Brazil, not one woman was elected to the national legislature in 1985. In sum, it must be concluded that, despite some not unimportant policy changes, 'the political representation of women ... has not improved substantially' (Jaquette, 1989:195): nowhere did the women's movement secure greater power or institutionalized participation of an enduring kind (Safa, 1990).[9]

The Fate of Social Movements and the Democratic Future

On the evidence of recent democratic transitions in Latin America it is now clear that 'social movements are unlikely to radically transform large structures of domination or dramatically expand elite democracies, certainly not in the short run' (Escobar and Alvarez, 1992:325). But it is argued that they still have an important role to play in democratizing social relations (see Chapter 3) and in mediating between local communities and political systems, so strengthening the connection between civil society and institutional politics (see Chapter 4). The demobilization and decline of the movements which follows democratic transition need not therefore mean the end of their political potential. New collective identities have been created. Civil society has been 'discovered' and transformed. Politics is more plural. Democracy is now valued as an end in itself.

However, this optimistic view depends on arguments of *longue durée*. The political impact of social movements is understood to be gradual and cumulative. State agencies and political parties slowly come to recognize the movements as legitimate players on the political scene, and to engage in dialogue with them. Social movements at the grassroots continue to search for ways to express and represent popular demands. And the many small contests and conflicts can and do add up to a more comprehensive challenge to traditional political practices. My own work on Spain and Mexico (Foweraker, 1989a; 1993) tends to support the argument that social movements are successful in changing popular perceptions, institutional cultures and political practices, even if these changes are unlikely to be sudden or dramatic. But doubts remain. On the one hand it seems important to distinguish between the myriad forms of cultural and political 'resistance' at local level (which have characterized popular culture since time immemorial) and contemporary social movements that aspire to make some impact on the political system overall. On the other, it is important for the shorter term to decide whether social movements act to deepen and defend precarious democratic arrangements, or whether they increase the threat of authoritarian reversal. More concretely, can social movements strengthen democracy 'while simultaneously challenging the exclusionary mechanisms of specific democratic institutions' (Barros, 1986:64)?

The question of exclusion is critical to an appreciation of the relationship between social movements and democracy in contemporary Latin America. Indeed the critique of current democratic arrangements as being 'elitist and unconnected with the lived experience of the mass of the population' has been characterized as the 'social movements perspective' (Whitehead, 1992:154). In the present context the clear predominance of 'elite' over 'popular' democracy is expressed in the strong adherence to neoliberal economic policies. It is argued that contemporarily only a neoliberal strategy can lead to the successful consolidation of democracy because the social democratic path is seen 'as hopelessly over-optimistic given the weak productive base' (Whitehead, 1992:156). Since the neoliberal approach has the clear advantage of being feasible, 'the choice would be between a stunted version of liberal democracy that works, or a generous vision of social democracy that remains a mirage (the Chilean Constitution of 1980 versus the Brazilian Constitution of 1988)' (Whitehead, 1992:154). But the problem with the neoliberal approach is that 'what can be consolidated by these means would seem to exclude many of the features commonly associated with full liberal democracy (high participation, authentic political choice, extensive citizenship rights)' (Whitehead, 1992:154). In other words this exclusionary model leads to 'a very partial form of democratic politics – a form of politics in which the involvement of some bears a direct relation to the limited or non-participation of others' (Held, 1992:20).

This partial form of democracy has been called the 'second best' outcome for the countries of Latin America. 'Reformist, populist or socialist projects had been attempted and had failed; reactionary authoritarian projects had also been attempted and had also failed' (Whitehead 1992:148). The result was 'democracy by default', or political systems which fail to consolidate or institutionalize democracy, and 'will not conform neatly to any of our theoretical or practical models of authoritarian and democratic regimes' (Malloy, 1987:252). In short there will be democratic advance and authoritarian retreat, and not 'a nice neat linear movement from one clear-cut regime type (authoritarian) to some other type (democratic)' (Malloy, 1987:251). However the limitations on democracy and, consequently, the indeterminacy of regime type, will vary from country to country: 'restrictions on national sovereignty; curtailment of political choice by market mechanisms; "facade" arrangements intended to project an external image of pluralism without disturbing traditional power relations; the persistence of undemocratic structures in rural areas; policy paralysis derived from fiscal crisis; misguided design of institutional arrangements; a fragmented civil society incapable of generating legitimacy or social consensus' (Whitehead, 1992:158). All these and further 'limitations' are possible, in any combination.

Although there is some evidence that these partial democracies are having some success in subordinating the armed forces to the rule of law, their lack of institutionalization is seen most flagrantly in their highly presidentialist forms of government and the rapid resort to arbitrary decision-making. This style of governance has been called 'delegative democracy' (O'Donnell, 1992) or 'democratic Caesarism', and is typical of these 'hybrid regimes that ... give the executive quasi-authoritarian power in times of crisis' (Malloy, 1987:257). What then matters is not the institutional form of political participation, but access to the executive and, whatever the specific configuration of the hybrid regime, what remains constant is 'the inclination ... to capture executive sources of benefits that flow more as patronage and privileges than as universal rights' (Malloy, 1987:252). In short, the partial democracies of Latin America merely pay lip-service to liberal values and democratic rights and continue to practise the politics of populism and clientelism. What is then required is 'a thorough examination of the relation between formal rights and actual rights, between commitments to treat citizens as free and equal and practices which do neither sufficiently' (Held, 1992:20). What this examination will reveal is that social movements still have a vital and specific role to play in securing democratic government. Whereas elite actors, party leaders and pressure groups target the executive and 'usually operate through parties and legislatures only to defend achieved privileges' (Malloy, 1987:252), social movements will continue to press for more popular participation in decision-making and a more positive application of democratic rights. Above all, social movements will mobilize to close the gap between the rhetoric and reality of citizenship, between the promise and the practice of democratic rights. Indeed, in the present context of partial democracy, the best working definition of a social movement is a popular organization which can make plausible claims to exercise a perceptible impact on the extension and exercise of the rights of citizenship.

Notes

Chapter 2 – Theories of Social Movements

1. In Habermas' language, the 'communicative action' which creates the lifeworld is displaced by the subsystems of action coordinated by money and power. In this perspective, social movements address issues of cultural reproduction and social integration, but are not concerned with social welfare and economic distribution as such.

2. A heavy emphasis on the stability of the social system made such movements marginal to functionalism. Structural Marxism only recognized such movements where 'objective' and 'subjective' factors coincided, or where social actors became class actors: national or gender struggles were seen as 'secondary' at best, or as symptoms of false consciousness of different kinds.

3. Touraine insisted on the essentially anti-institutional character of social movements. A genuine movement must be able to go beyond its immediate context and concerns, and to develop a systematic critique of the dominant structure of power. Cohen sees Touraine's approach as both narrow and unrealistic. Without a sense of strategic initiative (and of interaction with the institutional environment) it is difficult to see how social movements can achieve institutional change (see Chapter 4).

4. Tilly defines the nineteenth-century sense of social movement as 'a set of people who voluntarily and deliberately commit themselves to a shared identity, a unifying belief, a common program, and a collective struggle to realize that program' (Tilly, 1984:303). Although the sense is clear, it is doubtful if, by this definition, any social movement has ever existed anywhere in history.

5. My own account of the teachers' movement in Mexico (Foweraker, 1993) provides ample evidence to support this assertion.

6. The strong emphasis on the roles played by organization and leadership in making social movements strategically effective owes much to the theories of Max Weber and Robert Michels.

7. Included in the notion of 'structural location' would be prior contacts with movement members (social networks); member-

ship of other organizations; prior activism; and biographical availability (students, professionals) (McAdam, 1989).

8. This potential tautology also derives from one of the theory's main premises: since 'grievances' and mobilizing beliefs in general are ubiquitous, the real problem is to explain *how* not *why* protest is organized. The latent assumption here is that choosing to act must necessarily advance the actor's 'interests' (whatever they are). Piven and Cloward (1992) suggest that the evidence from the United States does not support the constant grievance assumption. If economic performance influences electoral politics, as it so clearly does, why should economic and social pressures not also affect collective action? Moreover they conclude that such pressures are in fact being reintroduced into resource mobilization theory, by the back door, in the form of 'suddenly imposed grievances' (Walsh, 1981) or 'public bads' (McAdam et al., 1988).

9. This applies a fortiori to game-theoretical analyses of competing players. The game of 'prisoners' dilemma', for example, assumes equal knowledge or equal ignorance on the part of the two players, and should not therefore be applied to the relationship between social movements and the state. This does not stop some theorists from doing so.

10. The essay by McAdam et al. referred to the collective behaviour approach (Blumer), the mass society approach (Arendt and Kornhauser), and the relative deprivation approach (Gurr).

11. These observations will seem unexceptional to anyone who has done empirical work on social movements; and the thought may occur (both here and elsewhere in the social movement literature) that a large theoretical hammer is being used against a rather small empirical nut.

12. As noted before, the exception for Habermas is feminism, which clearly has a 'dual logic': it not only seeks political inclusion and equal rights but also pursues identity, alternative values and an attack on male monopolies.

13. She concludes that 'for us, the traceless transformation of movements into bureaucratic political parties or lobbies remains both a negative and an avoidable model' (Cohen and Arato, 1992: 561).

14. This is not to deny that social actors have rational intentions, but rather to assert that the process of strategic choice itself can never be rational. Melucci recognizes that identity is a 'negotiated' result of 'complex interactions' (Melucci, 1988) but he still understands the process to be subject to conscious and directive decision-making. He finally remains insensitive to the unpredictable and genuinely contingent nature of identity.

15. In an earlier version Tilly added 'in the course of which those persons make publicly visible demands for changes in the distribution or exercise of power, and back those demands with public demonstrations of support' (Tilly, 1982).

16. Reviewing the literature on the civil rights movement in the United States, Cohen concludes that 'it was influence, not money or power, that was operative here' (Cohen and Arato, 1992:507).

17. Slater suggests that anti-centralism is the key element of many local and regional social movements, especially in the Andean countries. This is linked to the erosion of the state's legitimacy, and 'in several interior zones (of Peru and Colombia) the localized authority and coercive power of the state has been broken' (Slater, 1991:44).

18. Social movements have been around for a long time, especially in Mexico where the Revolution 'gave life to a political system that both legitimized and institutionalized collective organization and action' (Davis, 1992:402). Nor are they a new topic of social scientific inquiry. A bibliography published by the *Revista Mexicana de Sociología* (*Mexican Journal of Sociology*) in 1985 listed 372 articles and books published in Mexico on social movements between 1968 and 1984 alone (Davis, 1992:400). The point here – and it will be debated in detail in subsequent chapters – is that their 'newness' may lie in the form and quality of their relationship to the state.

19. This can be nicely illustrated by the rapid growth of urban associations in Brazil in the period 1979–81 which coincided precisely with both strong economic recession and a significant slackening of political controls. In the preceding period of economic growth and political repression the urban movements were far less dynamic.

20. Franco observes that all torturers were male, and were socialized by blood pacts and different kinds of initiation rite. Even their male victims were 'feminized' by being isolated and reduced to passive objects. Franco also asserts that the male leaders of revolutionary organizations like the Tupamaros never truly accepted female combatants, who were considered 'butches' rather than women.

21. One of the (necessary) fictions of this chapter is that Latin America can act analytically as an empirically coherent category. In fact, the economic, social and political variation within the continent is huge, and some of this variety will become apparent in subsequent chapters. Slater suggests the depth of the differences between national realities by referring to 'the reactionary despotism of the Central American region; the violent internal fragmentation of Colombian and Peruvian

societies; the fragile peripheral capitalist democracies of Argentina, Brazil, Chile and Uruguay, and the (post) revolutionary societies of Cuba and pre-1990 Nicaragua' (Slater, 1991:44).

Chapter 3 – The Sociology of Social Movements

1. At the same time he warned against the 'empiricist illusion'. Social movements could only be understood by 'selecting a general mode of analysis of social life on the basis of which a category of facts called social movements can be constituted' (Touraine, 1988:63).
2. The essay by Calderon et al. may be laudable in intent, but it seems to indulge in the most misleading kind of wishful thinking. At one point they ask, 'Who can deny the centrality of marginals in the political citizenry of the future?' It appears doubtful whether such queries are informed by processes of empirical research.
3. Lehmann provides a graphic account of Catholic base communities as 'micromobilization context': 'Catholic base communities are numerous, decentralized and small; they sprout up, decay and disappear. Some meet to read and comment on the Bible with or without priestly guidance, others are involved in development work, organizing the provision of sewage disposal or a community health project; some may be involved in the struggle for land, in the countryside or the city, or in conflicts over wages; and very often they are involved in the defence of human rights, as when members are taken to prison because of their political or semi-political involvement or, in the countryside, when they are victimized by landowners' (Lehmann, 1990b:135).
4. This refers to the European context where the one movement is equivalent to the 'period of historical creation that emerged in the 1960s and that had by the end of the 1980s largely been incorporated into established politics, in the guise of green parties, mainstream public interest organizations, women's studies departments, environmental bureaucracies etc.' (Eyerman and Jamison, 1991:91). In effect, this one movement was the student movement, and the 'new social movements provided specification, a kind of specialization to the rather overextended cosmological ambitions of the 1960s'.
5. Not all social movements in contemporary Europe are progressive. Many are better characterized as nationalistic, xenophobic, racist or fascist.
6. D'Anieri and Kier studied the Chartist movement, the Oneida Community and the West German Peace Movement in terms

of their goals, form, participants and values, before concluding that old and new movements look very similar indeed. Slater objects that 'the degree of comparability or continuity is considerably overdrawn, especially given the fact that the fundamentally different nature of state-society relations, within which and across which today's social movements act and develop, is left out of account' (Slater, 1991:59, f. 3). If Slater is right, differences in state-society relations are sufficient to differentiate social movements across time as well as across political cultures (from Europe or the United States to Latin America).

7. Weffort was making a general argument about the reconstruction of civil society under the military regime in Brazil. It was born of the widespread experience of fear in the context of family and friends. From there it spread first to the popular church, press and bar associations; and finally to unions, business groups and cultural activities.

8. At the highest level of abstraction Touraine argues that 'cultural orientations define the field of historicity, and they are shared by social actors, who fight over their control' (Touraine, 1988:8).

9. Piven and Cloward argue that resource mobilization theorists overstate the degree of organization necessary for collective protest. The 'lateral integration' that is supposed to be a prerequisite for protest is ubiquitous, but the protest itself is episodic and infrequent. The kind of mobilization that occurs in student protests or ghetto riots requires a bare minimum of contact and communication. Hence, 'organizational capacity does not predict anything' (Piven and Cloward, 1992:312). It may be objected that without some form of organization no movement will be able to conduct negotiations with other social forces or the state.

10. In Argentina the Church hierarchy was highly reactionary and the Church was therefore unprepared to support popular protest and social mobilization.

11. The proportion of wage earners in the economically active population of Chile declined from 53 per cent in 1971 to 38 per cent in 1982; while the proportion of the unemployed or occasionally employed with less than the minimum wage rose from 14 per cent in 1971 to 36 per cent in 1982 (Kirkwood, 1983).

12. However, since women have always been involved in community management, and to a lesser degree in negotiating on behalf of the community, it is readily admitted that many of their activities within the community should be classified as *pre-movement* rather than social movement proper.

13. These objectives might include the abolition of the sexual

division of labour, the attainment of political equality, freedom of choice, and adequate institutional guarantees against male violence. Demands arising from these objectives tend to be labelled 'feminist' (Molyneaux, 1985). More recently Molyneaux's typology has been criticized as too static: the key questions should be why certain objectives are chosen by particular organizations at specific moments, and how these objectives change over time.

14. In fact, *Poder Feminino* was anything but a feminist movement.

Chapter 4 – The Politics of Social Movements

1. 'Non-institutional collective action will tend to metamorphose into institutional action where the risks, for example of illegality, are lower. Furthermore, loose organizations demanding high degrees of commitment from members will give way to tighter more formal organizations where the organizational burdens will be taken over by "professionals" or quasi-professionals, and where the demands on grass-roots members will be restricted to occasional meetings, participation in collective action etc.' (Scott, 1991:113).

2. Melucci sees this as characteristic of the 'original' or traditional social movements in Europe, where, for example, 'industrial conflict was inextricably bound up with the national problem and with that of extending political rights to excluded social groups' (Melucci, 1988). In his view, however, the new social movements do not correspond to this image of social actors as historical agents marching towards a destiny of liberation (see Chapter 3).

3. In all these cases social movements arose from specific state initiatives to promote the top-down mobilization of social sectors which were previously excluded from politics. But the state may also promote mobilization more obliquely and as a contingent result of broader social and economic policies. For example, it has been noted that the numerically strongest and politically most effective women's movements in contemporary Latin America are to be found in Brazil, Peru and Mexico, where state policies have massively increased the presence of women in education, production and politics (Jaquette, 1989).

4. Mueller (1992) notes four key points in the process of 'micro-construction': the centrality of face-to-face interaction for constructing group loyalties; the support for or resistance to patterns of dominance and inequality in the interactional routines of everyday life; the organizational linkages between microlevel

interactions and the larger structures of community and networks; and the conflict or struggle that is critical in the reconstruction of cultural meanings and group loyalties.

5. By these means the state manipulates social movements in order to isolate them and confine them to local and discrete conflicts. It has been suggested that there may be hidden strength in this dispersion of the movements insofar as it diversifies movement strategy, complicates state cooptation and dilutes state influence (even if the state remains the primary point of reference for most movements) (Escobar and Alvarez, 1992). This may be wishful thinking. Social movements themselves nearly always pursue some kind of alliance strategy in an attempt to overcome their own isolation and fragmentation.

6. More particularly, 'just as civic leaders ... must acquiesce or actively participate in lending pre-existing structures to social change purposes, political authorities (those who can make binding decisions within geographical boundaries) can acquiesce or actively participate in making structures of state available to facilitate or constrain social movement mobilization' (McCarthy and Wolfson in Morris and Mueller, 1992:279).

7. Some commentators believe that the 'regulatory capacity' of the institutional context has to be fractured before social movements can influence the state. Since this occurs only during 'periods of profound social dislocation' it follows that the possibility of effective protest only arises very infrequently (Piven and Cloward, 1977:14). I make a different kind of argument later in this chapter.

8. By the end of the Echeverría period in Mexico (1970–6) there had been a huge increase in squatter settlements in the large cities, with land invasions being prepared carefully beforehand. In Monterrey in the north some 30 such settlements containing about 100,000 squatters came together to form the *Frente Popular Tierra y Libertad*. The Frente sought to take advantage of divisions between the governor of the state and the chief of police, and between the Monterrey business elite and the PRI government. Moreover, the alliance strategy of the Frente and organizations like the *Comite de Defensa Popular* in Durango and Chihuahua was successful in securing some degree of participation in local government decision-making.

9. The ABC triangle is formed by the three industrial townships of São Andres, São Bernardo and São Caetano, and is the heartland of São Paulo's heavy engineering and automobile plants.

10. Lowy notes that 'it is difficult to find analogues and equiva-

lents; from a historical standpoint, the example it most closely approaches would be the Independent Labour Party, the first English workers' party, formed in 1893 by a group of combative union leaders, socialist militants (including some Marxists), and Christian leftists, with the blessings of an ageing Engels' (Lowy, 1987:454).

11. At the end of the conflictual decade of the 1970s in Europe Suzanne Berger concluded that the anti-political actions of new social movements were directed as much against existing parties and interest groups as against capitalist society as such (Berger, 1979).

Chapter 5 – Social Movements and Democratic Transitions

1. The authors go on to ask, 'How else can one account for the worker's movement, civil rights movement, the women's movement, the ecology movement, regional struggles for autonomy, or any modern social movement?' (Cohen and Arato, 1992:295).

2. Democratic transitions express a wide variety of trajectories and outcomes. The role of social movements within them is conditioned by the specific rhythm of the 'protest cycle', the shape of the political opportunity structure, and the contingencies of strategic choice (see Chapter 2). By way of example, in Chile it took a long cycle of protest and a rising rhythm of social mobilization to create the political conditions for the plebiscite and the eventual return to democratic government, while in Argentina mass mobilization did not occur until elections had been announced and the transition itself was almost a foregone conclusion.

3. Weffort argues that both the concept and reality of civil society have been very tenuous compared to the strength of state traditions and myths in Brazil. The links between civil society and democracy were weak or deformed. Democracy was always seen as a 'means to power': 'the instrumental conception of democracy runs through our history like a curse' (Weffort, 1989:334). The rediscovery of civil society and associationalism were therefore essential to the reconstitution of a democratic political society.

4. Cathy Schneider reports this assertion of the president of a democratically elected neighbourhood council in Yungay, one of the urban districts of Santiago de Chile organized by the Chilean Communist Party (Schneider, 1992).

5. 'In modern civil society, rights are not only moral oughts, but also empower. Rights do not only individualize, they are also a medium of communication, association and solidarity. They

do not necessarily depoliticize; they can also constitute a vital connection between private individuals and the new public and political spheres in society and state' (Cohen and Arato, 1992:297).

6. Keck notes the massive expansion of the industrial working class in Brazil, and emphasizes that most of the workers belonged to a new generation that had grown up under military rule: 'the pre-1964 period was at most a childhood memory ... these young workers were building their organizations on the basis of experience gained under the authoritarian regime' (Keck, 1989:260).

7. In general 'the move to electoral parties with their less intense, more inclusive, more abstract form of political identification and their lower degree of direct participation tends to devalue and replace movements and associations with their more particular, but also more intense and participatory forms of organization' (Cohen and Arato, 1992:53).

8. Social movements in Argentina have found it very difficult to secure political representation within a weak political party system that has failed to mediate between the main 'economic corporate' groups of civil society and the government. Things may now be changing. The economic crisis and government austerity policies which have weakened the Peronist subculture and divided the labour movement may yet encourage a stronger party system. But social movements are unlikely to make much impact on the configuration of the system.

9. Sadly this is now true even of Nicaragua, where the women's movement had made very substantial advances. Women had accounted for about 30 per cent of the FSLN's armed combatants, and so had a clear expectation that the revolutionary government would address their concerns. Since women also made up the great majority of poorest Nicaraguans, they did benefit considerably from the government's general welfare and reform policies (including land reform), and the government also made men legally responsible for the welfare of their families, so furthering the cause of sexual equality (Molyneaux, 1985). But there were no constitutional or political guarantees for these advances, and most of them have since been reversed by economic and political crisis.

Bibliography

Alvarez, Sonia E. (1989) 'Women's Movements and Gender Politics in the Brazilian Transition', in Jaquette, Jane, ed., *The Women's Movement in Latin America: Feminism and the Transition to Democracy*, Unwin Hyman: Winchester, MA.

—— (1990) *Engendering Democracy in Brazil: Women's Movements in Transition Politics*, Princeton University Press: Princeton.

Archetti, E., ed. (1987) *Sociology of 'Developing' Societies: Latin America*, New York: Monthly Review Press.

Arizpe, Lourdes (1990) 'Foreword: Democracy for a Small Two-Gender Planet', in Jelin, Elizabeth, ed., *Women and Social Change in Latin America*, UNRISD/Zed Books: London.

Assies, Willem (1991) *To Get Out of the Mud: Neighborhood Associativism in Recife, 1964–1988*, CEDLA: Amsterdam. Latin American Studies 63.

Assies, Willem, Gerret Burgwal and Ton Salman (1991) *Structures of Power, Movements of Resistance: an Introduction to the Theories of Urban Movements in Latin America*, CEDLA: Amsterdam.

Banck, Geert A. (1990) 'Cultural Dilemmas behind Strategy: Brazilian Neighbourhood Movements and Catholic Discourse', *European Journal of Development Research* 2, 1.

Barbalet, J.M. (1988) *Citizenship: Rights, Struggle and Class Inequality*, Open University Press: Milton Keynes.

Barros, Roberto (1986) 'The Left and Democracy: Recent Debates in Latin America', *Telos*, no. 68 (Summer).

Berger, Johannes and Claus Offe (1982) 'Functionalism versus Rational Choice: Some Questions Concerning the Rationality of Choosing One or the Other', *Theory and Society* 11, 2.

Berger, Suzanne (1979) 'Politics and Anti-Politics in Western Europe in the Seventies', *Daedalus* (Winter).

Birnbaum, Pierre (1988) *States and Collective Action: The European Experience*, Cambridge University Press: Cambridge.

Blondet, Cecilia (1990) 'Establishing an Identity: Women Settlers in a Poor Lima Neighbourhood', in Jelin, Elizabeth, ed., *Women and Social Change in Latin America*, UNRISD/Zed Books: London.

Bobbio, Norberto (1989) *Democracy and Dictatorship*, Polity Press: Cambridge.

Boggs, Carl (1986) *Social Movements and Political Power – Emerging Forms of Radicalism in the West*, Temple University Press: Philadelphia.

Boschi, Renato (1984) 'On Social Movements and Democratization: Theoretical Issues', Occasional Paper, Stanford-Berkeley Joint Center for Latin American Studies (Spring).

—— (1987a) 'Social Movements and the New Political Order in Brazil', Wirth, John D., Edson de Oliveira Nunes and Thomas E. Bogenschild, eds, *State and Society in Brazil*, Westview Press: Boulder, CO.

—— (1987b) *A Arte de Associação: Política de Base e Democracia no Brasil*, Edicões Vertice e IUPERJ: São Paulo.

—— (1990) 'Social Movements, Party Systems and Democratic Consolidation: Brazil, Uruguay and Argentina', in Ethier, Diane, ed., *Democratic Transition and Consolidation in Southern Europe and Latin America and Southeast Asia*, Macmillan: London.

Bourdieu, Pierre and James S. Coleman (1991) *Social Theory for a Changing Society*, Westview Press: Boulder, CO.

Brand, Karl-Werner (1990) 'Cyclical Aspects of New Social Movements: Waves of Cultural Criticism and Mobilization Cycles of New Middle-class Radicalism', in Dalton, Russell and Manfred Kuechler, eds, *Challenging the Political Order: New Social Movements in Western Democracies*, Polity Press: Cambridge.

Brennan, Geoffrey and Loren E. Lomasky, eds (1989) *Politics and Process: New Essays in Democratic Thought*, Cambridge University Press: Cambridge.

Bresser Pereira, Luiz Carlos, José María Maravall and Adam Przeworski (1992) *Economic Reform in New Democracies*, Cambridge University Press: New York.

Bright, Charles and Susan Friend Harding, eds (1984) *Statemaking and Social Movements: Essays in History and Theory*, University of Michigan Press: Ann Arbor.

Brint, Michael (1991) *A Genealogy of Political Cultures*, Westview Press: Boulder, CO.

Brockett, Charles D. (1991) 'The Structure of Political Opportunities and Peasant Mobilization in Central America', *Comparative Politics* 23 (April).

Burdick, John (1992) 'Rethinking the Study of Social Movements: the Case of Christian Base Communities in Urban Brazil', in Escobar, Arturo and Sonia E. Alvarez, eds, *The Making of Social Movements in Latin America: Identity, Strategy, and Democracy*, Westview Press: Boulder, CO.

Caldeira, Teresa Pires de Rio (1990) 'Women, Daily Life, and Politics', in Jelin, Elizabeth, ed., *Women and Social Change in Latin America*, UNRISD/Zed Books: London.

Calderón, Fernando, ed. (1985) *Los Movimientos Sociales ante la Crisis*, CLACSO: Buenos Aires.

Calderón, Fernando and Elizabeth Jelin (1987) *Clases y Movimientos Sociales en America Latina*, CEDES: Buenos Aires.

Calderón, Fernando, Alejandro Piscitelli and José Luis Reyna
(1992) 'Social Movements: Actors, Theories, Expectations', in
Escobar, Arturo and Sonia E. Alvarez, eds, *The Making of
Social Movements in Latin America: Identity, Strategy, and
Democracy*, Westview Press: Boulder, CO.

Cardoso, Fernando Henrique (1986) 'La Democracia en las Socie-
dades Contemporaneas', Martín del Campo, Julio Labastida, ed.,
Los Nuevos Procesos Sociales y la Teoría Política Contemporánea,
UNAM/Siglo XXI: Mexico D.F.

Cardoso, Ruth Corrêa Leite (1983) 'Movimentos Sociais Urbanos:
Balanço Critíco', Sorj, Bernardo and Maria Herminia Tavares de
Almeida, eds, *Sociedade y Política no Brasil Pos-1964*, Editora
Brasiliense: São Paulo.

—— (1987) 'Movimentos Sociais na América Latina', *Revista
Brasileira de Ciencias Sociais* vol. 1, no. 3.

—— (1988) 'Os Movimentos Populares no Contexto da Con-
solidação da Democracia', Wanderley Reis, Fabio and Guillermo
O'Donnell, eds, *A Democracia no Brasil: Dilemas e Perspectivas*,
Edições Vertice: São Paulo.

—— (1992) 'Popular Movements in the Context of the Consoli-
dation of Democracy in Brazil', in Escobar, Arturo and Sonia
E. Alvarez, eds, *The Making of Social Movements in Latin
America: Identity, Strategy, and Democracy*, Westview Press:
Boulder, CO.

Castells, Manuel (1977) *The Urban Question: a Marxist Approach*, Edward Arnold: London.

—— (1982) 'Squatters and Politics in Latin America: a Comparative Analysis of Urban Social Movements in Chile, Peru
and Mexico', in Safa, Helen, ed., *Toward a Political Economy
of Urbanization in Third World Countries*, Oxford University
Press: New Delhi.

—— (1983) *The City and the Grassroots*, Edward Arnold: London.

Chant, Sylvia (1991) *Women and Survival in Mexican Cities:
Perspectives on Gender, Labour Markets and Low-income
Households*, Manchester University Press: Manchester.

Chinchilla, Norma Stoltz (1992) 'Marxism, Feminism, and the
Struggle for Democracy in Latin America', in Escobar, Arturo
and Sonia E. Alvarez, eds, *The Making of Social Movements
in Latin America: Identity, Strategy, and Democracy*, Westview
Press: Boulder, CO.

Chuchryk, P. (1989a) 'Subversive Mothers: the Women's Opposition to the Military Regime in Chile', Charlton, S.E. et al., eds,
Women, the State and Development, SUNY Press: Albany.

—— (1989b) 'Feminist Anti-Authoritarian Politics: the Role of
Women's Organizations in the Chilean Transition to Democracy', in Jaquette, Jane, ed., *The Women's Movement in Latin*

America: Feminism and the Transition to Democracy, Unwin Hyman: Winchester, MA.

CLACSO's Grupo de Trabajo 'Movimientos Sociales y Participación Popular' (1990) *Movimientos Sociales y Políticas: El Desafío de la Democracia en America Latina*, CES-CLACSO: Santiago.

Cohen, Jean L. (1985) 'Strategy or Identity: New Theoretical Paradigms and Contemporary Social Movements', *Social Research* 52, 4 (Winter).

Cohen, Jean and Andrew Arato (1992) *Civil Society and Political Theory*, MIT Press: Cambridge, MA.

Collier, Ruth B. (1982) 'Popular Sector Incorporation and Political Supremacy: Regime Evolution in Brazil and Mexico' in Hewlett, S.A. and R. Weinhert, eds, *Brazil and Mexico: Patterns of Late Development*, Institute for the Study of Human Issues: Philadelphia.

Connolly, William E. (1987) *Politics and Ambiguity*, University of Wisconsin Press: Madison.

Corcoran-Nantes, Yvonne (1990) 'Women and Popular Urban Social Movements in São Paulo, Brazil', *Bulletin of Latin American Studies* vol. 9, no. 2.

Cornelius, Wayne and Ann Craig (1984) *Politics in Mexico: an Introduction and Overview*, Center for U.S. Mexican Studies, University of California, San Diego. Reprint Series no. 1.

Costain, Anne N. (1992) *Inviting Women's Rebellion: a Political Process Interpretation of the Women's Movement*, Johns Hopkins University Press: Baltimore.

Crow, Graham (1989) 'The Use of the Concept of "Strategy" in Recent Sociological Literature', *Sociology* vol. 23, no. 1 (February).

Dahl, Robert A. (1971) *Polyarchy: Participation and Opposition*, Yale University Press: New Haven.

—— (1989) *Democracy and its Critics*, Yale University Press: New Haven.

Dalton, Russell J. and Manfred Kuechler, eds (1990) *Challenging the Political Order. New Social and Political Movements in Western Democracies*, Oxford University Press: New York.

D'Anieri, Paul, Claire Ernst and Elizabeth Kier (1990) 'New Social Movements in Historical Perspective', *Comparative Politics* vol. 22, no. 4, (July).

Davis, Diane E. (1989) Review of Eckstein *Power and Popular Protest*, *Journal of Interamerican Studies and World Affairs*, 31 (Winter).

—— (1992) 'The Sociology of Mexico: Stalking the Path not Taken', *Annual Review of Sociology* 18: 395–417.

Diamond, Larry, Juan J. Linz and Seymour Martin Lipset, eds

(1989) *Democracy in Developing Countries. Volume Four: Latin America,* Lynne Rienner Publishers: Boulder, CO.

Diniz, Eli, Renato Boschi and Renato Lessa (1989) *Modernização e Consolidação Democrática no Brasil,* Editora Vertice, IUPERJ: São Paulo.

Dix, Robert (1992) 'Democratization and the Institutionalization of Latin American Political Parties', *Comparative Political Studies* vol. 24, no. 2.

Dresser, Denise (1991) *Neopopulist Solutions to Neoliberal Problems: Mexico's National Solidarity Program,* Center for US–Mexican Studies, San Diego. Current Issue Briefs, 3.

Diamond, Larry (1989) 'Beyond Authoritarianism and Totalitarianism: Strategies for Democratization', *Washington Quarterly* vol. 12, no. 1.

Diani, Mario and Giovanni Lodi (1988) 'Three in One: Currents in the Milan Ecology Movement', in Klandermans, Bert, Hanspeter Kriesi and Sidney Tarrow, eds, *From Structure to Action: Comparing Movements Across Cultures,* International Social Movements Research vol. 1, JAI Press: Greenwich, CT.

Diani, Mario and Ron Eyerman (1992) *Studying Collective Action,* Sage: London.

Eckstein, Susan (1989) *Power and Popular Protest: Latin American Social Movements,* University of California Press: Berkeley.

Elster, Jon (1982) 'Marxism, Functionalism and Game Theory: the Case for Methodological Individualism', *Theory and Society* 11, 2.

Escobar, Arturo and Sonia E. Alvarez, eds (1992) *The Making of Social Movements in Latin America: Identity, Strategy, and Democracy,* Westview Press: Boulder, CO.

Ethier, Diane, ed. (1990) *Democratic Transition and Consolidation in Southern Europe, Latin America and Southeast Asia,* Macmillan: Basingstoke.

Evers, Tilman (1985) 'Identity: the Hidden Side of New Social Movements in Latin America', in Slater, David, ed., *New Social Movements and the State in Latin America,* CEDLA: Amsterdam.

Eyerman, Ron and Andrew Jamison (1991) *Social Movements: a Cognitive Approach,* Polity Press: Cambridge.

Fals Borda, Orlando (1986) 'El Nuevo Despertar de los Movimientos Sociales', *Revista Foro* vol. 1, no. 1 (September).

—— (1992) 'Social Movements and Political Power in Latin America', in Escobar, Arturo and Sonia E. Alvarez, eds, *The Making of Social Movements in Latin America: Identity, Strategy, and Democracy,* Westview Press: Boulder, CO.

Feijoó, Maria del Carmen (1989) 'The Challenge of Constructing Civilian Peace: Women and Democracy in Argentina', in

Jaquette, Jane, ed., *The Women's Movement in Latin America: Feminism and the Transition to Democracy*, Unwin Hyman: Winchester, MA.

Foucault, Michel (1977) *Discipline and Punish: the Birth of the Prison*, Pantheon Books: New York.

Foweraker, Joe (1981) *The Struggle for Land: a Political Economy of the Pioneer Frontier in Brazil*, Cambridge University Press: Cambridge.

—— (1987) 'Corporatist Strategies and the Transition to Democracy in Spain' *Comparative Politics*, vol. 20, no. 1 (October).

—— (1989a) *Making Democracy in Spain: Grass-roots Struggle in the South, 1955-1975*, Cambridge University Press: New York.

—— (1989b) 'Popular Movements and the Transformation of the System', in Cornelius, W., J. Gentleman and P. Smith, eds, *Mexico's Alternative Political Futures*, Center for US–Mexican Studies, University of California, San Diego.

—— (1993) *Popular Mobilization in Mexico: the Teachers' Movement 1977-1987*, Cambridge University Press: New York.

Foweraker, Joe and Ann Craig (1990) *Popular Movements and Political Change in Mexico*, Lynne Rienner Publishers: Boulder, CO.

Franco, Jean (1992) 'Gender, Death and Resistance: Facing the Ethical Vacuum', in Corradi, Juan E., Patricia Weiss Fagen and M.A. Garretón, eds, *Fear at the Edge*, University of California Press: Berkeley.

Friedman, Debra and Doug McAdam (1992) 'Collective Identity and Activism: Networks, Choices, and the Life of a Social Movement', in Morris, Aldon D. and Carol McClurg Mueller, *Frontiers in New Social Movement Theory*, Yale University Press: New Haven.

Fuentes, Marta and André Gunder Frank (1989) 'Ten Theses on Social Movements', *World Development* vol. 17, no. 2: 179–91.

Gamson, William A. (1975) *The Strategy of Social Protest*, Dorsey: Homewood, Ill.

—— (1992) 'The Social Psychology of Collective Action', in Morris, Aldon D. and Carol McClurg Mueller, eds, *Frontiers in New Social Movement Theory*, New Haven: Yale University Press.

Garretón, Manuel Antonio (1987) *Reconstruir la Política: Transición y Consolidación en Chile*, Editorial Andante: Santiago de Chile.

—— (1989a) *The Chilean Political Process*, Unwin Hyman: Boston.

—— (1989b) 'Popular Mobilization and the Military Regime in Chile: the Complexities of the Invisible Transition', in Eckstein, Susan, ed., *Power and Popular Protest*, University of California Press: Los Angeles.

—— (1991) 'Democratic Inauguration in Chile: from Pinochet to Aylwin', *Third World Quarterly* vol. 13.

Giddens, Anthony (1974) *New Rules of Sociological Method*, Hutchinson: London.

Gillespie, Charles Guy (1989) 'Democratic Consolidation in the Southern Cone and Brazil: Beyond Political Disarticulation?', *Third World Quarterly* vol. 11, no. 2 (April).

González, Mercedes de la Rocha and Augustín Escobar Latapí (1991) *Social Responses to Mexico's Economic Crisis of the 1980s*, Center for US–Mexican Studies, San Diego.

Gorz, André (1982) *Farewell to the Working Class*, South End Press: Boston.

Gramsci, Antonio (1973) *Selections from the Prison Notebooks*, Hoare, Q. and G.N. Smith, eds, Lawrence and Wishart: London.

Grzybowski, Cândido (1987) *Caminhos e Descaminhos dos Movimentos Sociais no Campo*, FASE (Federação de Orgões para Assistencia Social e Educacional): Rio; Vozes: Petrópolis.

Habermas, Jurgen (1973) *Legitimation Crisis*, Heinemann: London.

—— (1987) *The Philosophical Discourse of Modernity*, MIT Press: Cambridge, MA.

—— (1989) *The Structural Transformation of the Public Sphere*, Polity: Cambridge.

Hagopian, Francis (1990) 'Democracy by Undemocratic Means? Elites, Political Pacts and Regime Transition in Brazil', *Comparative Political Studies* vol. 23, no. 2.

Hannigan, John A. (1985) 'Alain Touraine, Manuel Castells and Social Movement Theory: a Critical Reappraisal', *Sociological Quarterly* 26.

Harvey, David (1989) *The Condition of Postmodernity*, Basil Blackwell: Oxford.

Held, David (1987) *Models of Democracy*, Polity Press: Cambridge.

—— (1989) *Political Theory and the Modern State*, Polity Press: Cambridge.

—— ed. (1991) *Political Theory Today*, Polity Press: Cambridge.

—— ed. (1992) 'Democracy: from City-states to a Cosmopolitan Order?', *Political Studies*, vol. XL, Special Edition on 'Prospects for Democracy'.

Higley, John and Richard Gunther (1992) *Elites and Democratic Consolidation in Latin America and Southern Europe*, Cambridge University Press: New York.

Hindess, Barry (1984) 'Rational Choice Theory and the Analysis of Political Action', *Economy and Society* vol. 13, no. 3.

Hirschman, Albert (1982) *Shifting Involvements: Private Interests and Public Action*, Princeton University Press: Princeton.

—— (1991) *The Rhetoric of Reaction*, Harvard University Press: Cambridge.

Hobsbawm, Eric J. (1983) 'Introduction: Inventing Traditions',

Hobsbawm, E.J. and T. Ranger, eds, *The Invention of Tradition*, Cambridge University Press: Cambridge.

Huntington, Samuel P. (1984) 'Will More Countries become Democratic?', *Political Science Quarterly* vol. 2 (Summer).

Inglehart, Ronald (1977) *The Silent Revolution: Changing Values and Political Styles among Western Publics*, Princeton University Press: Princeton.

Jaquette, Jane, ed. (1989) *The Women's Movement in Latin America: Feminism and the Transition to Democracy*, Unwin Hyman: Winchester, MA.

Jelin, Elizabeth, ed. (1985) *Los Nuevos Movimientos Sociales* (2 vols), Centro Editor de América Latina: Buenos Aires.

—— (1987) *Ciudadanía e Identidad: Las Mujeres in los Movimientos Sociales Latino-Americanos*, UNRISD: Geneva.

—— (1990) *Women and Social Change in Latin America*, UNRISD/ Zed Books: London.

Jenkins, J. Craig (1983) 'Resource Mobilization Theory and the Study of Social Movements', *Annual Review of Sociology* 9. Special Edition.

Jonas, Susanne and Nancy Stein, eds, (1990) *Democracy in Latin America: Visions and Realities*, Bergin and Garvey: New York.

Journal of Democracy (1992), special edition on 'Capitalism, Socialism and Democracy'.

Kaase, Max (1990) 'Social Movements and Political Innovation', in Dalton, Russell and Manfred Kuechler, *Challenging the Political Order: New Social Movements in Western Democracies*, Polity Press: Cambridge.

Karl, Terry Lynn (1990) 'Dilemmas of Democratization in Latin America', *Comparative Politics* vol. 23, no. 1.

Karnen, Hartmut (1987) 'Movimentos sociais: revolução no cotidiano', in Scherer-Warren, Ilse and Paulo J. Krischke, eds, *Uma Revolução no Cotidiano? Os novos movimentos sociais na América Latina*, São Paulo: Editora Brasilense.

Keane, John, ed. (1988) *Civil Society and the State*, Verso: London.

Keck, Margaret (1989) 'The "New Unionism" in the Brazilian Transition', Stepan, Alfred, ed., *Democratizing Brazil*, Oxford University Press: New York.

Kirkwood, Julietta (1983) 'Women and Politics in Chile', *International Social Science Journal* no. 35.

Kitschelt, Herbert P. (1986) 'Political Opportunity Structures and Political Protest: Anti-Nuclear Movements in 4 Democracies', *British Journal of Political Science* 16 (January).

—— (1990) 'New Social Movements and the Decline of Party Organization', in Dalton, Russell and Manfred Kuechler, *Challenging the Political Order: New Social Movements in Western Democracies*, Polity Press: Cambridge.

Klandermans, Bert, Hanspeter Kriesi and Sidney Tarrow, eds (1988) *From Structure to Action: Comparing Movements Across Cultures*, International Social Movements Research vol. 1, JAI Press: Greenwich, CT.

Klandermans, Bert (1990) 'Linking the "Old" and "New": Movement Networks in the Netherlands', in Dalton, Russell and Manfred Kuechler, *Challenging the Political Order: New Social Movements in Western Democracies*, Polity Press: Cambridge.

—— (1992) 'The Social Construction of Protest and Multiorganizational Fields', in Morris, Aldon D. and Carol McClurg Mueller, *Frontiers in New Social Movement Theory*, New Haven: Yale University Press.

Kowarick, Lúcio (1982) 'O Preço do Progresso: Crescimento Económico, Pauperização e Espoliação Urbana', Moisés, J.A. ed., *Cidade, Povo e Poder*.

—— (1988) *As Lutas Sociais e a Cidade*, Paz e Terra: São Paulo.

Kriesi, Hanspeter (1988) 'Local Mobilization for the People's Petition of the Dutch Peace Movement', in Klandermans, Bert, Hanspeter Kriesi and Sidney Tarrow, eds, *From Structure to Action: Comparing Movements Across Cultures*, International Social Movements Research vol. 1, JAI Press: Greenwich, CT.

Krischke, Paulo J. (1987) 'Movimentos sociais e transição política: contribuições da democracia de base', in Scherer-Warren, Ilse and Paulo Krischke, eds (1987) *Uma Revolução no Cotidiano? Os Novos Movimentos Sociais na América Latina*, Brasilense: São Paulo.

Laclau, Ernesto (1977) *Politics and Ideology in Marxist Theory*, Verso: London.

—— (1985) 'The Hegemonic Form of the Political: a Thesis', Abel, C. and C. Lewis, eds, *Latin America: Economic Imperialism and the State*, Athlone Press: London.

Laclau, Ernesto and Chantal Mouffe (1985) *Hegemony and Socialist Strategy: Towards a Radical Democratic Politics*, Verso: London.

Lash, Scott and John Urry (1984) 'The New Marxism of Collective Action: a Critical Analysis', *Sociology* vol. 18, no. 1.

Lehmann, David, ed. (1990a) Special Edition *European Journal of Development Research* vol. 2, no. 1 (June).

—— (1990b) *Democracy and Development in Latin America: Economics, Politics and Religion in the Post-War Period* (Chs 3–5), Temple University Press: Philadelphia.

Levine, Andrew, Elliott Sober and Erik Olin Wright (1987) 'Marxism and Methodological Individualism', *New Left Review* no. 162 (March–April).

Levine, Daniel (1988) 'Paradigm Lost: Dependency to Democracy', *World Politics* vol. XL, no. 3 (April).

Lipsky, Michael (1968) 'Protest as a Political Resource', *American Political Science Review* 62, no. 4.

Lo, Clarence Y. (1992) 'Communities of Challengers in Social Movement Theory', in Morris, Aldon D. and Carol McClurg Mueller, eds, *Frontiers in New Social Movement Theory*, New Haven: Yale University Press.

Lomnitz, Larissa and Ana Melnick (1991) *Chile's Middle Class: a Struggle for Survival in the Face of Neoliberalism*, Lynne Rienner Publishers: Boulder, CO.

Lowy, Michael (1987) 'A New Type of Party: the Brazilian PT', *Latin American Perspectives* vol. 14, no. 4 (Fall).

Machado da Silva, Luis A. and Alicia Ziccardi (1983) 'Notas para uma discussão sobre "Movimentos Sociais Urbanos" ' in Machado da Silva et al., eds, *Movimentos Sociais, Minorías Étnicas, e Outros Estudos*, ANPOCS: Brasília.

Mainwaring, Scott (1987) 'Urban Popular Movements, Identity, and Democratization in Brazil', *Comparative Political Studies* 20, 2 (July).

—— (1988) 'Political Parties and Democratization in Brazil and the Southern Cone', *Comparative Politics* vol. 21.

—— (1989) 'Grassroots Popular Movements and the Struggle for Democracy: Nova Iguaçú', in Stepan, A., ed., *Democratizing Brazil*, Oxford University Press: New York.

—— (1992) 'Transitions to Democracy and Democratic Consolidation: Theoretical and Comparative Issues', in Mainwaring, Scott, Guillermo O'Donnell and J. Samuel Valenzuela, eds, *Issues in Democratic Consolidation: the New South American Democracies in Comparative Perspective*, University of Notre Dame Press: South Bend, IN.

Mainwaring, Scott and Eduardo Viola (1984) 'New Social Movements, Political Culture and Democracy: Brazil and Argentina in the 1980s', *Telos* 61 (Fall).

Mainwaring, Scott, Guillermo O'Donnell and J. Samuel Valenzuela, eds (1992) *Issues in Democratic Consolidation: the New South American Democracies in Comparative Perspective*, University of Notre Dame Press: South Bend, IN.

Malloy, James (1987) 'The Politics of Transition in Latin America', in Malloy, J.M. and M.A. Seligson, eds, *Authoritarians and Democrats: Regime Transition in Latin America*, University of Pittsburgh Press: Pittsburgh.

Mann, Michael (1987) 'Ruling Class Strategies and Citizenship', *Sociology* vol. 21, no. 3 (August).

Marshall, T.H. (1965) 'Citizenship and Social Class', in T.H. Marshall *Class, Citizenship and Social Development*, Anchor Books: Garden City, New York.

Marx Ferree, Myra (1992) 'The Political Context of Rationality:

Rational Choice Theory and Resource Mobilization', in Morris, Aldon D. and Carol McClurg Mueller, eds, *Frontiers in New Social Movement Theory*, New Haven: Yale University Press.

Marx, Gary T. (1974) 'Thoughts on a Neglected Category of Social Movement Participant: the Agent Provocateur and Informant', *American Journal of Sociology* vol. 80, no. 2

—— (1979) 'External Efforts to Damage or Facilitate Social Movements: Some Patterns, Explanations, Outcomes, and Complications', in McCarthy, John D. and Mayer N. Zald, eds, *The Dynamics of Social Movements: Resource Mobilization, Social Control and Tactics*, Winthrop Publishers: Cambridge, MA.

Marx, Gary T. and James L. Wood (1975) 'Strands of Theory and Research in Collective Behavior', *Annual Review of Sociology* vol. 1.

Marx, Karl (1981) *Early Writings*, Penguin Books: Harmondsworth.

Massolo, Alejandra (1989) 'Mujer y Política Urbana: la Desconocida de Siempre, la Siempre Presente', Foro *Mujeres e Políticas Públicas, Mujeres en Acción Social*, Fundación F. Ebert: Mexico (Abril).

Massolo, A. and Lucila Díaz Ronner (1983) 'La Participación de las Mujeres en los Movimientos Sociales Urbanos', Programa Integrado de Estudios sobre la Mujer: El Colegio de Mexico (27 julio).

Matta, Roberto da (1987) 'The Quest for Citizenship in a Relational Universe', in Wirth, John D., Edson de Oliveira Nunes and Thomas E. Bogenschild, eds, *State and Society in Brazil: Continuity and Change*, Westview Press: Boulder, CO.

Maybury-Lewis, Bjorn (1991) *The Politics of the Possible: the Growth and Development of the Brazilian Rural Workers' Trade Union Movement, 1964–85*, PhD thesis: Columbia University.

McAdam, Doug (1989) 'The Biographical Consequences of Activism', *American Sociological Review* vol. 54 (October).

McAdam, Doug, John McCarthy and Mayer Zald (1988) 'Social Movements', in *Handbook of Sociology*, Neil Smelser, ed., Sage: Newbury Park, CA.

McCarthy, John D. and Mayer N. Zald (1973) *The Dynamics of Social Movements: Resource Mobilization, Social Control and Tactics*, Winthrop Publishers: Cambridge, MA.

McCarthy, John and Mark Wolfson (1992) 'Consensus Movements, Conflict Movements, and the Cooptation of Civic and State Infrastructures', in Morris, Aldon D. and Carol McClurg Mueller, eds, *Frontiers in New Social Movement Theory*, Yale University Press: New Haven.

Melucci, Alberto (1985) 'The Symbolic Challenge of Contemporary Movements', *Social Research* vol. 52, no. 4 (Winter).

—— (1988) 'Getting Involved: Identity and Mobilization in Social Movements', in Klandermans, Bert, Hanspeter Kriesi and Sidney Tarrow, eds., *From Structure to Action: Comparing Movements Across Cultures*, International Social Movements Research vol. 1, JAI Press: Greenwich, CT.

—— (1989) *Nomads of the Present: Social Movements and Individual Needs in Contemporary Society*, Temple University Press: Philadelphia.

Michels, Robert (1949) *Political Parties*, Free Press: Glencoe, Ill.

Mills, C. Wright (1959) *The Sociological Imagination*, Oxford University Press: New York

Meyer, Lorenzo (1991) 'La Prolongada Transición Mexicana: del Autoritarismo hacia Donde?', *Revista de Estudios Políticos* no. 74. Nueva Época: Madrid.

Moira, L. (1991) 'Notas sobre la Transición Chilena', *Revista de Estudios Políticos* no. 74 (October–December).

Moisés, José Alvaro (1981) 'O Estado, as Contradições Urbanas e os Movimentos Sociais', in Moisés et al., eds, *Cidade, Povo e Poder*, Paz e Terra: Rio de Janeiro.

—— (1982) 'What is the Strategy of the New Syndicalism?', *Latin American Perspectives* vol. IX, no. 4 (Fall).

Moisés, José Alvaro et al. (1977) *Contradições Urbanas e Movimentos Sociais*, Paz e Terra: Rio de Janeiro.

Molyneaux, Maxine (1985) 'Mobilization without Emancipation? Women's Interests, the State and Revolution in Nicaragua', *Feminist Studies* vol. 11, no. 2.

—— (1990) 'The "Women Question" in the Age of Perestroika', *New Left Review* no. 183.

Moore Jr., Barrington (1973) *Social Origins of Dictatorship and Democracy: Lord and Peasant in the Making of the Modern World*, Penguin Books: Harmondsworth.

Moctezuma, Pedro (1984) 'El Movimiento Urbano Popular Mexicano', *Nueva Antropología* vol. VI, no. 24.

Moreira Alves, Maria Helena (1984) 'Grassroots Organizations, Trade Unions and the Church: a Challenge to the controlled Abertura in Brazil', *Latin American Perspectives* vol. 11, no. 1.

—— (1985) *State and Opposition in Military Brazil*, University of Texas Press: Austin.

Morris, Aldon D. and Cedric Herring (1987) 'Theory and Research in Social Movements: a Critical Review', *Annual Review of Political Science*, vol. 2.

Morris, Aldon D. and Carol Mueller, eds (1992) *Frontiers in Social Movement Theory*, Yale University Press: New Haven, CT.

Moser, Caroline (1987) 'The Experiences of Poor Women in Guayaquil', in Archetti, E., ed., *Sociology of 'Developing' Societies: Latin America*, New York: Monthly Review Press.

Mouffe, Chantal (1988) 'Hegemony and New Political Subjects: Toward a New Concept of Democracy', in Nelson, C. and L. Grossberg, eds, *Marxism and the Interpretation of Culture*, University of Illinois Press: Chicago.

Mueller, Carol McClurg (1992) 'Building Social Movement Theory', in Morris, Aldon D. and Carol McClurg Mueller, eds, *Frontiers in New Social Movement Theory*, Yale University Press: New Haven, CT.

Munck, Gerardo (n.d.) *Rethinking Democracy 'from Below': Toward a Theory of Social Movements*, mimeo.

Munck, Ronaldo (1984) 'Urban Social Movements: Labour in Argentina and Brazil', in Munck, R., ed., *Politics and Dependency in the Third World: the Case of Latin America*, Zed Press: London.

—— (1989) *Latin America: the Transition to Democracy*, Zed Press: London.

Nunes, Edison and Pedro Jacobi (1983) 'Movimentos Populares Urbanos, Participação e Democracia', Machado da Silva et al., eds, *Movimentos Sociais, Minorías Étnicas e Outros Estudos*, ANPOCS: Brasília.

Oberschall, Anthony (1973) *Social Conflict and Social Movements*, Prentice Hall: Englewood Cliffs, NJ.

O'Connor, James (1973) *The Fiscal Crisis of the State*, St Martin's Press: New York.

O'Donnell, Guillermo (1984) 'Democracia en la Argentina Micro y Macro', in Oszlak, Oscar, ed., *'Proceso', Crisis y Transición Democrática*, Centro Editor de América Latina: Buenos Aires.

—— (1992a) 'Delegative Democracy?', *Working Paper* no. 172, Helen Kellogg Institute for International Studies, University of Notre Dame.

—— (1992b) 'Transitions, Continuities and Paradoxes', in Mainwaring, Scott, Guillermo O'Donnell, and J. Samuel Valenzuela, eds, *Issues in Democratic Consolidation: the New South American Democracies in Comparative Perspective*, University of Notre Dame Press: South Bend, IN.

O'Donnell, Guillermo and Philippe Schmitter (1986) *Transitions from Authoritarian Rule (vol. 4) Tentative Conclusions about Uncertain Democracies*, Johns Hopkins University Press: Baltimore, MD.

Offe, Claus (1985) 'New Social Movements: Challenging the Boundaries of Institutional Politics', *Social Research* 52, 4 (Winter).

—— (1990) 'Reflections on the Institutional Self-transformation of Movement Politics: A Tentative Stage Model', in Dalton, Russell and Manfred Kuechler, eds, *Challenging the Political Order: New Social Movements in Western Democracies*, Polity Press: Cambridge.

Offe, Claus and Helmut Wiesenthal (1985) 'Two Logics of Collective Action', in Offe, Claus, ed., *Disorganized Capitalism*, MIT Press: Cambridge, MA.

Olson, Mancur (1965) *The Logic of Collective Action*, Harvard University Press: Cambridge, MA.

Oszlak, Oscar (1987) 'Privatización Autoritária y Recreación de la Escena Publica', in Oszlak, O., ed., *'Proceso', Crisis y Transición Democrática*, Centro Editor de América Latina: Buenos Aires.

Pansters, Wil (1986) 'Urban Social Movements and Political Strategy in Latin America', *Boletín de Estudios Latinoamericanos y del Caribe*, no. 41 (December).

Pérez Arce, Francisco (1990) 'The Enduring Union Struggle for Legality and Democracy', in Foweraker, Joe and Ann Craig, eds, *Popular Movements and Political Change in Mexico*, Lynne Rienner Publishers: Boulder, CO.

Pérez Díaz, Víctor (1987) *El Retorno de la Sociedad Civil*, IEE: Madrid.

Piven, Frances Fox and Richard A. Cloward (1977) *Poor People's Movements: Why They Succeed, How They Fail*, Pantheon Press: New York.

—— (1992) 'Normalizing Collective Protest', in Morris, Aldon D. and Carol McClurg Mueller, eds, *Frontiers in New Social Movement Theory*, Yale University Press: New Haven.

Pizzorno, Alessandro (1978) 'Political Exchange and Collective Identity in Industrial Conflict', in Crouch, C. and A. Pizzorno, eds, *The Resurgence of Class Conflict in Western Europe since 1968*, Macmillan: London (vol. 2).

—— (1985) 'On the Rationality of Democratic Choice', *Telos* 63 (Spring).

Przeworski, Adam (1985) 'Marxism and Rational Choice', *Politics and Society* 14, 4.

—— (1986) 'Some Problems in the Study of the Transition to Democracy', in O'Donnell, G., P. Schmitter and L. Whitehead, eds, *Transitions from Authoritarian Rule: Comparative Perspectives*, Johns Hopkins University Press: Baltimore.

Radcliffe, Sarah et al. (1993) *Viva: Women and Popular Protest in Latin America*, Routledge: London.

Ramírez Saiz, Juan Manuel (1987) *Política Urbana y Lucha Popular*, Universidad Autónoma de México, Xochimilco, Mexico City.

Rodriguez, V. and P. Ward (1991) 'Opposition Politics, Power and Public Administration in Urban Mexico', *Bulletin of Latin American Research* vol. 10, no. 1.

Rucht, Dieter (1990) 'The Strategies and Action Repertoires of New Movements', in Dalton, Russell and Manfred Kuechler, eds, *Challenging the Political Order: New Social Movements in Western Democracies*, Polity Press: Cambridge.

Sader Emil org (1987a) *Movimentos Sociais na Transição Democrática*, Cortez Editora: São Paulo.

—— (1987b) 'The Workers' Party in Brazil', *New Left Review* no. 165 (September–October).

Safa, Helen (1990) 'Women's Social Movements in Latin America', *Gender and Society* vol. 4, no. 3.

Schmitter, Philippe (1974) 'Still the Century of Corporatism?', *Review of Politics* 36.

Scherer-Warren, Ilse and Paulo Krischke (1987) *Uma Revolução no Cotidiano? Os Novos Movimentos Sociais na América do Sul*, Brasilense: São Paulo.

Schneider, Cathy (1992) 'Radical Opposition Parties and Squatters Movements in Pinochet's Chile', in Escobar, Arturo and Sonia E. Alvarez, eds, *The Making of Social Movements in Latin America: Identity, Strategy, and Democracy*, Westview Press: Boulder, CO.

Schuurman, Frans (1989) 'Urban Social Movements: between Regressive Utopia and Socialist Panacea', in Schuurman, F. and T. Van Naersen, eds, *Urban Social Movements in the Third World*, Routledge: New York.

Scott, Alan (1991) *Ideology and Social Movements*, Allen & Unwin: London.

Servolo de Medeiros, Leonilde (1989) *Historia dos Movimentos Sociais no Campo*, FASE: Rio de Janeiro.

Share, Donald and Scott Mainwaring (1986) 'Transitions through Transaction: Democratization in Brazil and Spain', in Selcher, W., ed., *Political Liberalization in Brazil*, Westview: Boulder, CO.

Silva, Juan and Frans Schuurman (1989) 'Neighborhood Associations in Buenos Aires: Contradictions within Contradictions', in Schuurman, F. and T. Van Naersen, eds, *Urban Social Movements in the Third World*, Routledge: New York.

Slater, David (1985) *New Social Movements and the State in Latin America*, CEDLA: Amsterdam.

—— (1991) 'New Social Movements and Old Political Questions Rethinking State–Society Relations in Latin American Development', *International Journal of Political Economy* vol. 21 (1) (Spring).

Snow, David, E. Burke Rochford, Steven K. Worden and Robert D. Benford (1986) 'Frame Alignment Processes, Micromobilization, and Movement Participation', *American Sociological Review* 51.

Snow, David A. and Robert D. Benford (1992) 'Master Frames and Cycles of Protest', in Morris, Aldon D. and Mueller, Carol McClurg, eds, *Frontiers in New Social Movement Theory*, Yale University Press: New Haven.

Soto, Orlando Nunez (1989) 'Social Movements in the Struggle for

Democracy, Revolution, and Socialism', *Rethinking Marxism* vol. 2, no. 1 (Spring).

Souza Martins, José de (1989) *Caminhada no Chão da Noite: Emancipação Política e Libertação nos Movimentos Sociais do Campo*, Editora Hucitec: São Paulo.

Stepan, Alfred, ed. (1988) *Democratizing Brazil*, Oxford University Press: New York.

Sternbach, N., M. Navarro-Aranguren, P. Chuchryk and S. Alvarez (1992) 'Feminisms in Latin America: from Bogotá to San Bernardo', *Signs* vol. 17, no. 2.

Stevens, Evelyn P. (1985) 'Mexico in the 1980s: from Authoritarianism to Power-sharing', in Wiarda, H.J. and H.S. Klein, eds, *Latin American Politics and Development*.

Street, Susan (1991) 'Movimientos Sociales y el Analisis del Cambio Sociopolítico en México', *Revista Mexicana de Sociología* Año LIII, no. 2.

Strong, Tracy B. (1992) *The Self and the Political Order*, Basil Blackwell: Oxford.

Tamayo, Jaime (1987) *Movimientos Sociales: Ensayos, Textos, Documentos*, CISMoS, Universidad de Guadalajara.

Tarrow, Sidney (1987) 'Between Moments of Madness and Ages of Contention: Cycles of Protest in Democratic States', Panel on *Dictatorships, Democracies and Opposition Movements*, APSA Annual Meeting, Chicago (September).

—— (1988a) 'National Politics and Collective Action: Recent Theory and Research in Western Europe and the United States', *Annual Review of Sociology* 14.

—— (1988b) 'Old Movements in New Cycles of Protest: The Career of an Italian Religious Community', in Klandermans, Bert, Hanspeter Kriesi and Sidney Tarrow, eds, *From Structure to Action: Comparing Movements Across Cultures*, International Social Movements Research vol. 1, JAI Press: Greenwich, CT.

—— (1989) 'Struggle, Politics and Reform: Collective Action, Social Movements, and Cycles of Protest', Western Societies Program Occasional Paper no. 21, Center for International Studies, Cornell University.

—— (1990) 'The Phantom of the Opera: Political Parties and Social Movements of the 1960s and 1970s in Italy', in Dalton, Russell and Manfred Kuechler, eds, *Challenging the Political Order: New Social Movements in Western Democracies*, Polity Press: Cambridge.

—— (1991) 'Aiming at a Moving Target: Social Science and the Recent Rebellions in Eastern Europe', *PS: Political Science and Politics* XXIV (1 March).

—— (1992) 'Mentalities, Political Cultures, and Collective Action Frames: Constructing Meanings through Action', in Morris,

Aldon D. and Carol McClurg Mueller, eds, *Frontiers in New Social Movement Theory*, Yale University Press: New Haven.

Taylor, Verta and Nancy Whittier, (1992) 'Collective Identity in Social Movement Communities: Lesbian Feminist Mobilization', in Morris, Aldon D. and Carol McClurg Mueller, eds, *Frontiers in New Social Movement Theory*, Yale University Press: New Haven.

Telles, Vera da Silva (1987) 'Movimentos sociais: reflexões sôbre a experiencia dos anos 70', in Scherer-Warren, Ilse and Paulo Krischke, eds, *Uma Revolução no Cotidiano*.

Thompson, E.P. (1974) *The Making of the English Working Class*, Penguin Books: Harmondsworth.

Tilly, Charles (1978) *From Mobilization to Revolution*, Prentice-Hall: Englewood Cliffs.

—— (1979) 'Repertoires of Contention in America and Britain' in Zald, Mayer and John McCarthy, eds, *Social Movements in an Organizational Society*, Transaction: New Brunswick, NJ.

—— (1982) 'Britain Creates the Social Movement', in Cronin, J.E. and J. Schneer, eds, *Social Conflict and the Political Order in Modern Britain*.

—— (1984) 'Social Movements and National Politics', in Bright, W. and S. Harding, eds, *State Building and Social Movements*, University of Michigan Press: Ann Arbor.

—— (1985) 'Models and Realities of Popular Collective Action', *Social Research* vol. 52, no. 4.

—— (1990) *Coercion, Capital and European States AD 990–1990*, Basil Blackwell: Oxford.

Tilly, Charles, Louise Tilly and Richard Tilly (1975) *The Rebellious Century: 1830–1930*, Harvard University Press: Cambridge, MA.

Touraine, Alain (1985a) *The Voice and the Eye: an Analysis of Social Movements*, Cambridge University Press.

—— (1985b) 'An Introduction to the Study of Social Movements', *Social Research* vol. 52, no. 4 (Winter).

—— (1987) *Actores Sociales y Sistemas Políticos en América Latina*, PREALC (Programa Regional del Empleo para América Latina y el Caribe)/OIT: Santiago de Chile.

—— (1988) *The Return of the Actor: Social Theory in Post-Industrial Society*, University of Minnesota Press: Minneapolis.

—— (1989) *Palavra e Sangue: Política e Sociedade na América Latina*, Universidade Estadual de Campinas: São Paulo.

Trejo, Raúl (1987) *Insurgencia, Convergencia y Movilización*, IIS UNAM: Mexico D.F.

Turner, Bryan S. (1986) *Citizenship and Capitalism: the Debate over Reformism*, Allen and Unwin: Boston.

Unger, Roberto M. (1987) *False Necessity: Anti-Necessitarian Social*

Theory in the Service of Radical Democracy, Cambridge University Press: Cambridge.

Valenzuela, M. (1990) 'Mujeres y Política: Logros y Tensiones en el Processo de Redemocratización', *Proposiciones* no. 18.

Viola, Eduardo and Scott Mainwaring (1985) 'Transitions to Democracy: Brazil and Argentina in the 1980s', *Journal of International Affairs* vol. 38, no. 2.

Wagner, Carlos (1988) *A Saga do João sem Terra,* Editora Vozes: Petrópolis.

Walsh, Edward J. (1981) 'Resource Mobilization and Citizen Protest in Communities around Three Mile Island', *Social Problems* 29: 1–21.

Wanderley Reis, Fabio (1988) 'Partidos, Ideologia e Consolidação Democrática', Wanderley Reis, Fabio and Guillermo O'Donnell, eds, *A Democracia no Brasil: Dilemas e Perspectivas,* Vertice: São Paulo.

Weber, Max (1966) *The Theory of Social and Economic Organization,* Talcott Parsons, ed., Free Press: New York.

Weffort, Francisco (1984) *Por Que Democracia?,* Brasiliense: São Paulo.

——— (1989) 'Why Democracy?', in Stepan, Alfred, ed., *Democratizing Brazil,* Oxford University Press: New York.

Whitehead, Laurence (1992) 'The Alternatives to Liberal Democracy: a Latin American Perspective', *Political Studies* vol. XL. Special Edition on 'Prospects for Democracy', Held, D., ed.

Wiarda, Howard J. and Herbert S. Klein (1985) *Latin American Politics and Development,* Westview: Boulder, CO.

Wilkinson, Paul (1971) *Social Movement,* Macmillan: London.

Wilson, Frank L. (1990) 'Neo-corporatism and the Rise of New Social Movements', in Dalton, Russell and Manfred Kuechler, eds, *Challenging the Political Order: New Social Movements in Western Democracies,* Polity Press: Cambridge.

Zald, Mayer and Michael Berger (1987) 'Social Movements in Organizations: Coup d'Etat, Bureaucratic Insurgency and Mass Movement', in Zald, Mayer and John McCarthy, eds, *Social Movements in an Organizational Society,* Transaction Books: New Brunswick/Oxford.

Zermeño, Sergio (1987) 'La Democracia como Identidad Restringida', *Revista Mexicana de Sociología* vol. 49, no. 4 (October).

Index